We dedicate this tome to all of those who came before us. They lived, they loved and they died. But, they made us the people we are today and we are most grateful for being their children.

"Girls Are Mighty Poor Property"
The Hicks Family of Wayne County, North Carolina

By The Hicks Cousins

©2018 The Scuppernong Press

First Printing

The Scuppernong Press
PO Box 1724
Wake Forest, NC 27588
www.scuppernongpress.com

Cover and book design by Frank B. Powell, III

All rights reserved

Printed in the United States of America

No part of this book may be reproduced or transmitted in any form or by any means, electronic or mechanical, including photocopying, recording, or by any information and storage and retrieval system, without written permission from the editor and/or publisher.

International Standard Book Number
    ISBN 978-1-942806-15-8

Library of Congress Control Number: 2018937666

"Girls Are Mighty Poor Property"

The Hicks Family of Wayne County, North Carolina

The Hicks Cousins

Wake Forest, NC
www.scuppernongpress.com

Chapters

Introduction 1

Origins 3

Herrings 5

Rapers 9

Robert Raper 11

Scotts 13

James E. Hicks 21

Papa Frank and Mama Ellen 23

Inez Isadora Hicks 37

Allen Milton Hicks 41

John Andrew Hicks 47

Ava Frances Hicks 51

Otto Frank Hicks 59

William Casper Hicks 65

George Appells Hicks 69

Mary Ellen Hicks 71

Recipes 75

Family Tree 107

Introduction

By our second annual cousins' reunion in 2016, hearing all the stories being told, someone stated we should write them down. For after all, if they die with us, they will be gone forever and our stories need to be preserved for future generations.

Being a publisher, I knew a book would not be a problem, all I needed was for the stories to be written down and e-mailed to me. And, of course, I would need photos to help illustrate our stories.

As for the title, *"Girls Are Mighty Poor Property,"* seems a strange and chauvinistic title for the 21st Century. Well you had to have known our grandfather, T. Frank Hicks or Papa Frank as we all called him. I only knew him as an old man. He was almost blind, deaf as a post, and stubborn, hard-headed, feeble and cantankerous. All his children helped look after him and Mama Ellen, but his main help was Aunt Inez and Aunt Ava along with Aunt Inez's youngest daughter, Georgia.

All three were present at the homeplace one day helping him when he made the statement, "you know, girls are mighty poor property." Of course, they chided him about his statement, telling him he would be in a mighty tough spot without his girls. But, I'm sure he didn't care.

We can only speculate on the reasons, but I can only suppose it was because he had five sons and they all worked on the farm with him while the girls worked in the house with their mother. But whatever the reason, everyone laughed it off and it became another family story told over and over again. And we even told it outside our family!

So, Papa Frank's statement just seemed to be the perfect title for our family history.

There are many more stories and reminiscences on the following pages. On behalf of all my cousins, I hope you enjoy our efforts and pass on our family history to future generations so they will know a little about the ones who came before them.

— *Frank B. Powell, III*

Origins

Hicks Name Meaning

English: patronymic from Hick 1. This is a widespread surname in England, and is common in the southwest and southern Wales. Dutch and German: patronymic from Hick. Compare Hix.

Name Distribution of Hicks Families

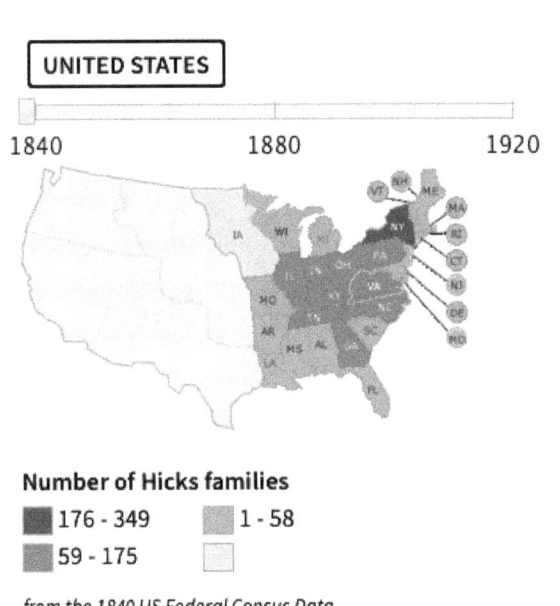

from the 1840 US Federal Census Data

The earliest records of the Hicks name in this country are found around 1620. It is thought they came from the British Isles. Records show Hicks settled up and down the east coast of what would become the United States. From there, they migrated south and westward.

Herrings

Herring Name Meaning

English, Scottish, Dutch, and German: metonymic occupational name for a herring fisher or for a seller of the fish, Middle English hering, Dutch haring, Middle High German hærinc. In some cases it may have been a nickname in the sense of a trifle, something of little value, a meaning which is found in medieval phrases and proverbial expressions such as 'to like neither herring nor barrel', i.e. not to like something at all. German: habitational name from Herringen in Westphalia. Dutch: from a personal name, a derivative of a Germanic compound name with the first element hari, heri 'army'. Jewish (Ashkenazic): variant spelling of Hering.

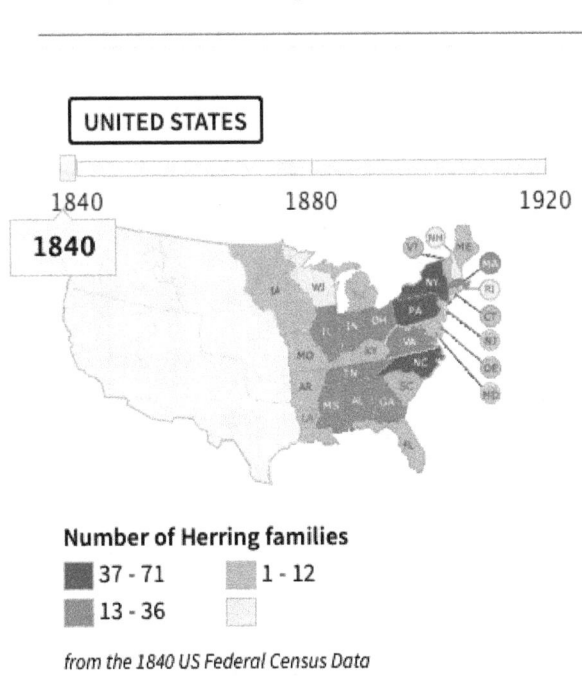

Name Distribution of Herring Families

from the 1840 US Federal Census Data

1929 Herring Reunion

Attending the 1929 Deems Herring Reunion were from left first row, Agelea Herring holding Bagnard Herring, Cleburn Herring, George Herring, Jr., Allen Griffin, Albis Hicks, Kate Mozingo, **Casper Hicks**, Geneva Hicks, **George Hicks**, **Mary Ellen Hicks**, Otto Griffin. Second Row, Retha Sloan, Effie Hicks holding Virginia Hicks, Deems Herring, Mary Porter Herring holding Joe Mozingo, Margaret Davenport, Victor Herring, Celiel Wiggs, **Otto Hicks**. Third Row, Zona Herring, Charlie Herring, Mary Herring, Edgar Herring, Deems Wiggs, Dixie Wiggs. Fourth Row, Bryant Mozingo, Grace Mozingo, Rosa Parker, George Herring, Lillian Herring, Dorothy ———, George Ora Wiggs holding Dorothy Wiggs, Marion Sloan, Nellie H. Sloan, Frank Parker. Fifth Row, **Ava Hicks**, Bertie Griffin, Charlie Hicks, Rex Wiggs, Robert Sloan, Ernest Herring, **Ellen Hicks**, Frank Parker, Robert Sloan, Joe Griffin holding Kenneth Griffin, **Frank Hicks**, Jeff Parker. Sixth Row, **Inez Hicks**, Denver Hicks, Charlie Hicks. Seventh Row, Nova Wiggs, Glenn Wiggs, **Milton Hicks**, Margaret Davenport and son.

Rapers

Raper Name Meaning

English (Yorkshire): variant of Roper. In southern dialects of English, Old English -a- became Middle English -o-, whereas in Yorkshire -a- was preserved and gave rise to this form of the surname. Possibly also an altered spelling of German Röper or Röber (see Roeber).

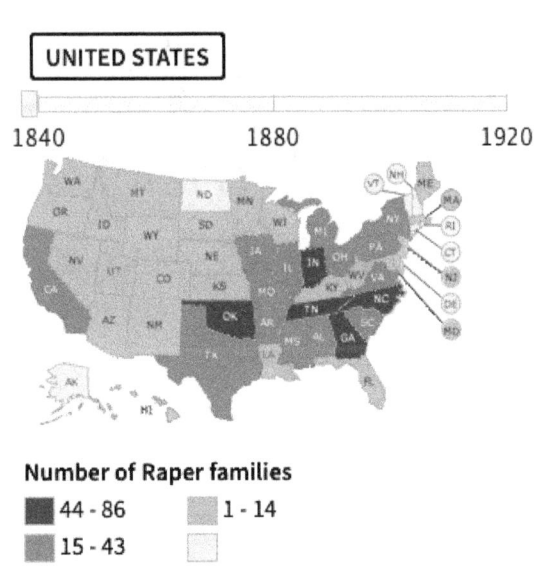

from the 1920 US Federal Census Data

Robert Raper

Robert Raper, one of the great-great-great-great grandfathers of the Hicks Cousins, was born in 1757 in Pasquotank County, NC, and was not educated.

He enlisted on April 6, 1776, as a private, for three years under a recruiting officer named Captain Edward Veal. The recruits were marched to New Bern and placed in Captain Robert Fenner's company after the election of officers. They were assigned to the Second North Carolina Regiment under Colonel Alexander Martin and Colonel John Fatton. They went down to Charleston for about a year and then proceeded overland to Philadelphia and came under the command of General George Washington. They participated at the Battle of Brandywine on September 11, 1777, and at Germantown on October 4, 1777.

Micajah Whitley of Wayne County, who had served in the Tenth North Carolina Regiment, testified in 1822 on Raper's pension application that he had known Raper when they passed the terrible winter at Valley Forge together.

The Second North Carolina fought at the Battle of Monmouth on June 28, 1778, and soon marched down to Charleston and were placed under the command of Benjamin Lincoln. About this time he served under Captains Charles Stewart and Thomas Evans. Raper and Micajah Whitley were captured there on May 12, 1780, and the former made his escape after two months and a day and went home to Pasquotank County.

He engaged in planting and was listed in Perquimans County in 1790 with two sons under sixteen, three daughters, a wife and one slave. He was living in Nash County, apparently what is now the western part of Wilson County on August 12, 1822, when he applied for a pension for his Revolutionary service. He had also lived across Contentnea Creek in Johnston County for about eight years.

He died on May 8, 1836.

Source: *The Heritage of Johnston County, North Carolina, 1985*

Scotts

Scott Name Meaning

English: ethnic name for someone with Scottish connections. Scottish and Irish: ethnic name for a Gaelic speaker.

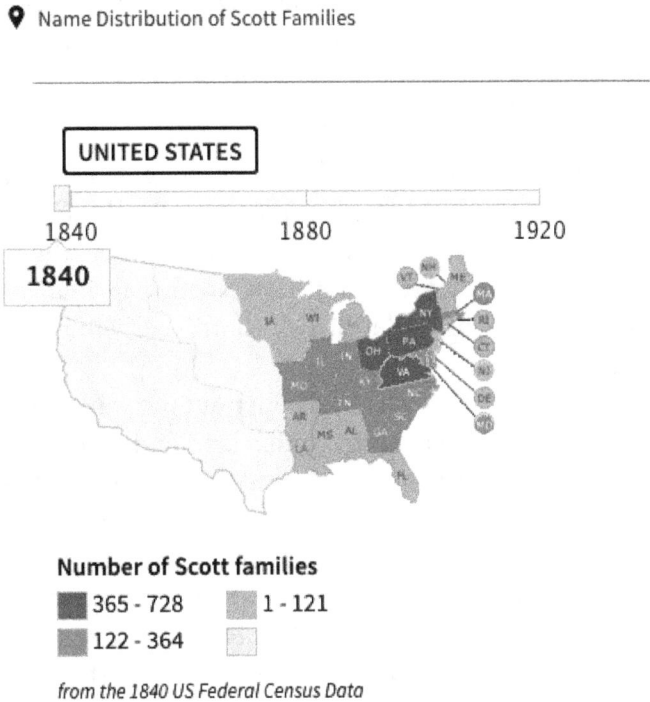

from the 1840 US Federal Census Data

The Ulster Scots, also called Ulster-Scots people or, outside the British Isles, Scots-Irish, are an ethnic group in Ireland, found mostly in the Ulster region and to a lesser extent in the rest of Ireland. Their ancestors were mostly Protestant Lowland Scottish migrants, the largest numbers coming from Galloway, Lanarkshire, Renfrewshire, Ayrshire and the Scottish Borders, with others coming from further north in the Scottish Lowlands and, to a much lesser extent, from the Highlands.

These Scots migrated to Ireland in large numbers both as a result of the government-sanctioned Plantation of Ulster, planned process of colonization which took place under the auspices of James VI of Scotland and I of England on land confiscated from members of the Gaelic nobility of Ireland who fled Ulster and as part of a larger migration or unplanned wave of settlement.

Ulster Scots emigrated onwards from Ireland in significant numbers to what is now the United States and to all corners of the then-worldwide British Empire. Scotch-Irish (or Scots-Irish) is a traditional term for Ulster Scots who emigrated to North America.

* * * *

Brothers Thomas and Andrew Scott fought at the Battle of Moore's Creek Bridge, in present day Pender County, under Richard Caswell on February 27, 1776. This little-known battle was very important as it kept North Carolina, and the South, from falling under British control early in the Revolutionary War.

The two brothers served throughout the war years and returned home and acquired much land and children.

Andrew Scott is the great-great-great-great-great grandfather of the Hicks Cousins. Andrew's grandfather Talbot Scott immigrated from Scotland to the northern coast of Virginia in 1681. After his death, his son James sold the land in Virginia and moved to Rowan County, NC. His sons, Thomas and Andrew later moved to Wayne County near Belfast about 1769.

Source: *The Heritage of Wayne County 1982*

* * * *

The day Granny Scott died we were all there because we liked to watch Mama Ellen feed her. Mama Ellen took real good care of her mother. Myself, Frank, Branda, Phyllis and Diane were there and Aunt Ava came in. Sometimes Aunt Ave came to help. But this morning she came in and took Granny Scott's hand and said "Granny's dead!" When she said that, the whole room exploded! Us kids ran off — there were bicycles in the yard, I don't even know which one I got on!

—*Ray Hicks*

An early visit to Pikeville
Mae Britt recalls 1913 trip

By Dennis Mathes
Staff Writer

Mount Olive resident Mae Britt doesn't remember much about her grandfather, John A. Scott, "He was a good fella," she said. "Big, fat. He was jolly. Everybody liked him." Scott, who died in 1918, will be featured along with several prominent Pikeville residents in the town's community building, which will be dedicated to the town as a museum later this year.

Scott's picture will hang in the museum. Mrs. Britt said he lived around Pikeville his entire life. He ran a saloon on East Railroad Street.

"He was born west of Pikeville," Mrs. Britt said. "The old Scott cemetery is out there close to where he was born, There's the prettiest old house down there to be sure.

"He farmed," she said. "He had a big farm. But he run that saloon." She laughed. "I don't know nothing about that only know they said he did, and I saw him on the other side of the street."

Mrs. Britt still has the keys to the saloon with Scott's name and the address on them.

Mrs. Britt was born in 1910. The first time she saw her grandfather in Pikeville was 1913.

"I'd seen him lots of times, but that's the first time I can remember going to Pikeville, seeing Pikeville," she said. "Granny (Mary Lee Hales) Starling had come to visit us on the other side of Clinton, and I come back home with her on the train. I can remember crossing the Cape Fear River. It was a covered bridge at that time.

"She had a horse and buggy and she'd get them hitched up and she'd go wherever she wanted to. So we got to Pikeville that day, and I saw grandpa coming down the street. I was holding her hand just as good. When I saw him, boy, I jerked a loose and I went running. He held his arms out like that, and I just went right up in them. I can see it just as good now."

Mrs. Britt said she remembers staying with Scott and her grandmother, Jane Frances Raper Scott.

"In the daytime, We would stay in the kitchen at the other end of the house, and after supper, we would go to the front part of the house," she said. "As you'd come in the door, he had a great big iron safe. And he had an arp. He would play that, and then he would want me to roll over on the floor, turn somersets.

"Then he wanted me to get up there and sit in his lap, hug his neck, and say, 'How much you love me?' I said, 'A bushel and a peck and a little bit in the gourd neck.' And then he would go to the closet and get that box of candy and give me one stick of peppermint candy."

Mrs. Britt was born four miles west of Pikeville. Her mother, Sue Ida Scott Starling, was Scott's youngest child. "She picked cotton, and granny would bring the dinners down there to the field to them, and they didn't even come to the house," Mrs. Britt said. "They had to pick 100 pounds before he'd give them any money."

Mrs. Britt's uncle and Scott's brother, Britian Scott, was the sheriff of Wayne County for many years. He also lived in Pikeville.

After her grandfather died, Mrs. Britt's family moved to the Mt. Carmel community. She visited Pikeville often. What was Pikeville like 70 years ago?

"Near about like it is now," she said. It's not growed too much. And they did have an old school, the big school. Mama had to walk two miles to Pikeville to school."

Mrs. Britt still has several relatives in Pikeville, and she learned about the museum from them.

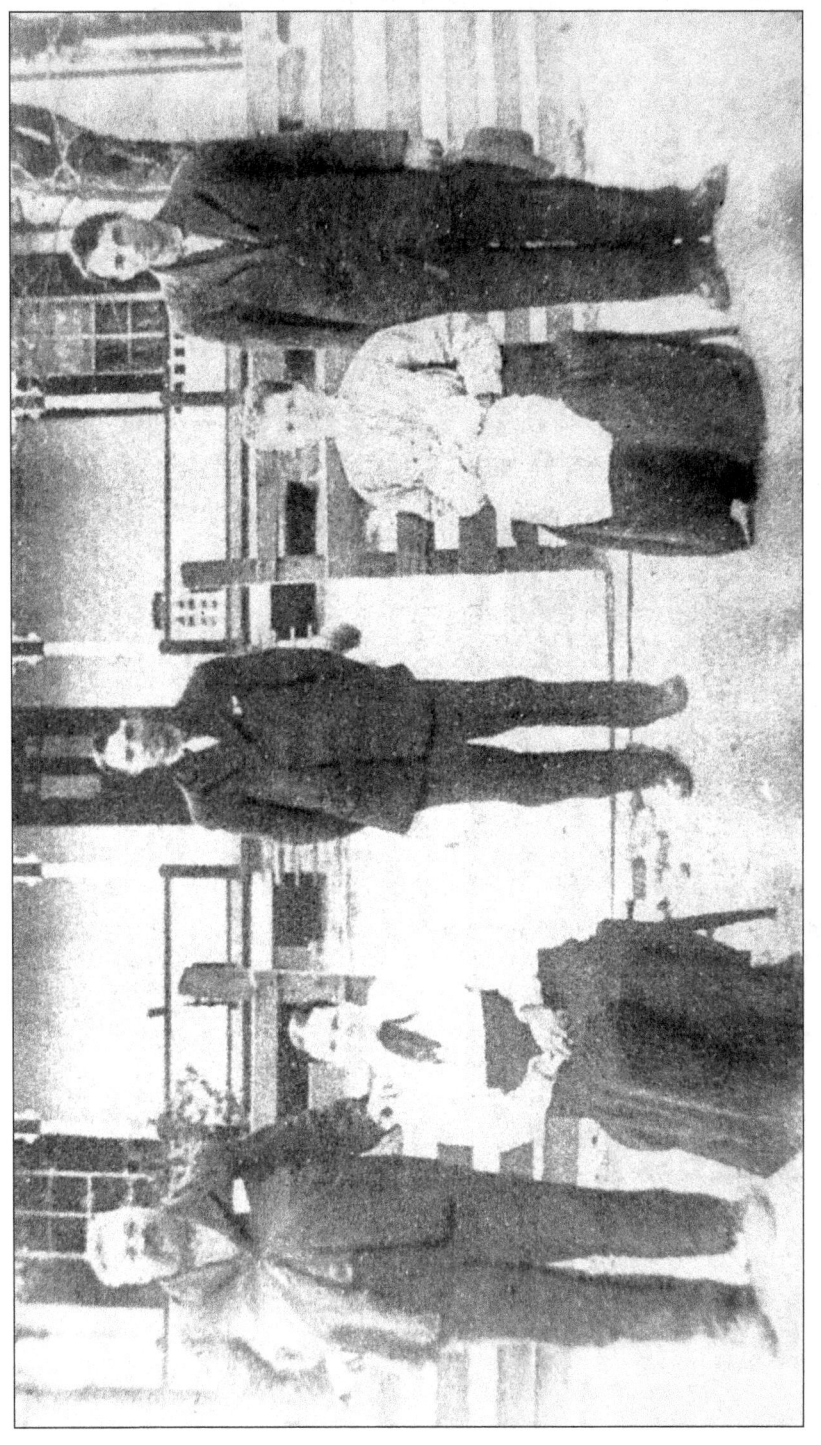

It was in the early 1900s when this family photo of relatives of Mount Olive resident Mae Britt was taken. From left, Mrs. Britt's grandparents, John Andrew Scott and Frances Raper Scott, her uncle, Probate Scott, her aunt, Nannie Dean Scott, her cousin Clarabelle Scott, and her uncle, Robert Emmett Scott.

*Frances Raper Scott and John Andrew Scott
on their wedding day, September 25, 1881.*

Mama Ellen (oldest) with her siblings, Bud, Robert and Ida Scott.

James E. Hicks

James E. Hicks was born in March 1840 in Wake County. He married Lucinda Herring in Wayne County on February 10, 1876. They had five children, Charles Denver born in 1877, James William born in 1879, Tavie Frank born in 1881, Rayford George born in 1883 and Lucinda born in 1887.

He enlisted in the 8th South Carolina Infantry on January 6, 1861, and served in this unit until he enlisted as a private in Orange County, NC, in the 13th Battalion NC Infantry on February 24, 1862 for the War. Was present or accounted for until transferred to Company A, 66th Regiment North Carolina Troops, October 2, 1863.

Reported present or accounted for through November 30, 1863. Reported on duty as a teamster from December 1, 1863 through October 30, 1864. No further records found. His pension application states he served with this regiment until the surrender of General Johnston in April 1865.

The 66th Regiment NC Troops participated in garrison duty in Eastern North Carolina until sent to the Army of Northern Virginia arriving on May 13, 1864 at Petersburg, VA.

They were at the following battles: Bermuda Hundreds, VA; Cold Harbor, VA; the siege of Petersburg, VA until December 22, 1864, when they were sent to Wilmington to help in the defense of Fort Fisher. Then they were at Kinston on March 7, 1865, and the Battle of Wise Forks, at the Battle of Bentonville March 19-21, 1865. They were with General Johnston on the withdrawal to Smithfield, Raleigh and Greensboro. They surrendered on April 26, 1865.

He applied for a NC Soldier's Pension on June 17, 1901, because he was unable to do manual labor.

He applied again on July 4, 1904, at 67 years of age. Living in Pikeville, NC, and unable to make a living by manual labor because of Brights disease and old age.

He died on June 7, 1907, and is buried in the Pikeville, NC, City Cemetery.

— *Frank B. Powell, III*

Papa Frank and Mama Ellen sometime in the 1950s.

Papa Frank and Mama Ellen

According to family traditions my grandfather Tavie Frank Hicks, was of Irish descent. He was born on September 6, 1881, the son of James E. (1847-1907) and Lucinda Herring Hicks James. A teamster during the War Between the States, worked for the railroad in Durham. He later moved his family to the Grantham area to farm. His wife died when Frank was just a young boy and he married his second wife, Mary Byrd. My grandfather always spoke very highly of his stepmother.

He had three brothers: Charles Denver (1877-1945); James William (1879-1945); and Rayford George (1883-1958), a sister, Lucinda died very young.

As a young man he moved to northern Wayne County and rented a farm. During this time he met and married a young school teacher, Mary Ellen Scott (August 30, 1882-February 5. 1975) on October 18, 1905. She was the daughter of John A. and Frances Raper Scott. John Scott was a merchant in Pikeville and owned the Scott Plantation. His brother, Britton Scott, served as Wayne County Sheriff from 1894-1900.

Frank Hicks was a magistrate, a farmer, operator of a sawmill and a cotton gin. Through hard work and his wife's support, he was able to buy property and eventually had considerable holdings.

In 1918 Frank and Ellen built a new home in the Mt. Carmel Community. He cut timber and sawed it at the sawmill which he operated with Robert Talton and Robert Scott, Ellen's brother. The house was one of the first in the area to have electric lights, indoor plumbing and a telephone.

Frank Hicks was a leader in his community and church. He served on the school board at Mt. Carmel School and was superintendent of the Mt. Carmel Methodist Church for more than fifty years. He also taught church school for a number of years. Frank and his family have been instrumental in the growth and beautification of the church.

Frank and Ellen had eight children: Inez I. (November 20, 1906) married David Leo Smith; Allen Milton (March 3,

1908) married Mabel Christine Lee; John Andrew (April 7, 1909) married Mary Noble Sasser; Ava Francis (September 20. 1910) married Walton Alex Aycock; William Casper (April 3, 1917) married Geraldine Forehand: Otto Frank (April 20, 1915) married Doris Lee Smith; George Appells (November 21, 1921) married Elizabeth Ann Parker; and Mary Ellen (September 6, 1922) married Frank Bishop Powell, Jr.

Frank Hicks is fondly remembered by his many descendants as being a colorful and unforgettable character, One had to admire his stubbornness and his struggle to maintain his independence in spite of declining health in his later years. Long after his friends had retired to their rocking chairs, he was still walking several miles each day, gardening, and driving his automobile at a reckless speed despite his failing eyesight In fact, his children had to insist he stop driving; nevertheless, he still looked forward to going into Pikeville to visit old friends and could be found waiting on the front porch around three o'clock. He would always treat his "chauffeur for the day" to a drink at the local drug store. He made it a point to pay for the drink, but he only would pay five cents for a drink even though the price had doubled, He claimed it was only worth five cents and his son, who owned the drug store, humored him.

He greatly admired Harry Truman. Like Truman, he wasn't a man of fancy words, but he had strong political and religious convictions. For instance, he advised his children, when they were courting, that anyone not a Democrat or a Methodist was "a son of a gun."

His long life can be attributed to the strong moral convictions and regimented schedules as follows: he had his meals at the same time every day, eating only in moderation; retired early and rose early each day; never acknowledged daylight savings time: and wouldn't venture from Wayne County unless he was assured of being home before the six o'clock news. He also thought that granddaughters weren't as desirable as grandsons; consequently, it was considered a waste of money to send them to college.

T. Franks Hicks died on April 25, 1970, and is buried in the Pikeville Cemetery. His memory still lives strong through the retelling of colorful anecdotes about him by his family and friends.

— *Branda Hicks Lane*

* * * *

Papa Frank had a big orchard with fruit frees and pecan trees. He also grew huckleberries, strawberries and grapes. I never asked Mother for a snack because I could go to the orchard and find something good to eat.

Papa Frank also had bee hives in the orchard. He would put on a big hat with netting and gloves to collect the honey. I can still picture him with the smoker chasing the bees away. Later the honey was delicious with one of Mama Ellen's hot biscuits. Living next door to your grandparents had many advantages.

— *Branda Hicks Lane*

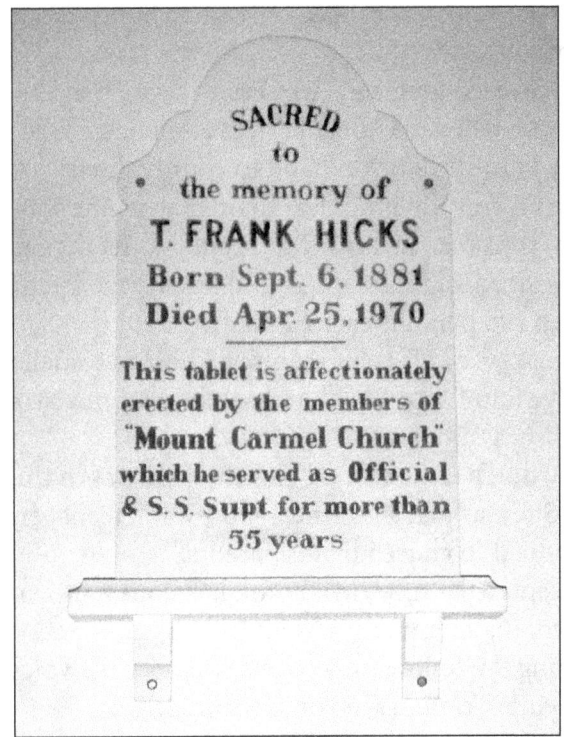

Mt. Carmel Church has had one superintendent 45 Years

Gene Roberts, Jr.
News-Argus Staff Writer

Forty-five years is a long time in the life of any man.

It is longer still in service as Sunday School superintendent of the same church.

But for Frank Hicks, for forty-five years superintendent at the Mount Carmel Methodist Church Sunday School, it has not seemed long at all.

"To say it has been a long time would be to admit I'm getting old," says Mr. Frank, "and besides, I've enjoyed every minute of it."

Members of his Sunday School think that Mr. Frank's service is a record for Wayne County and perhaps for the state. They are even more certain that his attendance is record setting. Mr. Frank has missed only three Sundays since he assumed office.

"I discovered long ago," Mr. Frank says, "that the only way a superintendent can expect perfect attendance is to let the members know he'll be on hand to county them."

From an enrollment of less than 25 when he was first elected to the office in 1911, Mr. Frank has let the Sunday School to an enrollment of 142 and an average attendance of more than 100 persons each Sunday.

"Almost every pleasant memory I hold is somehow connect with Mount Carmel Church of the Mount Carmel community," Mr. Frank says.

"Why the first time I ever saw my wife was in this church in 1895. She was just a girl then and I was a teenager who had been prodded to church by his parents."

And since that time, Mr. Frank has done a little prodding of his own. If a member is absent from Sunday School, sometime during the following week he will hear the voice of Mr. Frank saying, "We missed you on Sunday."

Sunday School Record – Frank Hicks, for forty-five years Sunday School Superintendent of the Mount Carmel Methodist Church, may hold a record as the North Carolina superintendent with the longest time in continuous service. The superintendent is shown above studying his Sunday School lesson.

    His insistence on perfect attendance sometimes led to concern among his eight children who often questioned why they could not occasionally miss a Sunday to take a weekend trip. "But I told them that a man who takes an office has a duty to those who elect him. No man wants an undependable leader," Mr. Frank said.

Six of his eight children are still attending Sunday School at Mount Carmel. "And the other two are attending regularly in other communities," Mr. Frank says with certitude.

In addition to his duties as superintendent, Mr. Frank has also doubled a teacher of the Adult Class for the past thirty years. "I have found that the old saying is true. The more I have put into the church the more I have gained from it."

As to whether he eventually plans to retire, Mr. Frank has a positive answer. "If they continue to want me, I hope to be holding the office for forty-five more years."

— From the *Goldsboro News-Argus*, September 27, 1956

Leader in the Mount Carmel Community

Rural Lady of the Week
Mrs. Frank Hicks Devotes Time to Church and Clubs

By Carl Bottoms
News-Argus Farm Editor

Mrs. Frank Hicks was born and reared in the Mount Carmel Church community and has devoted most of her life to making it a better place in which to live.

Mrs. Hicks attended school at Mount Carmel during the time there was a school located there. When she reached what was then high school, she attended school at Pikeville.

Following her graduation Mrs. Hicks taught school for three years. She was a teacher at Saulston School. She recalls how cold it was in the one-room frame building with only a few windows. Her students would take turns going out and gathering wood for the fire, she said. The students of today could not even imagine how it was in those days to get an education, Mrs. Hicks added.

There was one thing which may have been in favor of the students: then school was for only four months each year. Most of this time was during the winter months when there was little work to do on the farm.

Leader in the Mount Carmel Community — *Mrs. Frank Hicks who has done much to improve the Mount Carmel Methodist and the community in which she lives displays one of her prize winning begonias. She is an active member of the church and a charter member of the Home Demonstration club in that community.*

Most of the free time Mrs. Hicks has had aside from rearing eight children has been spend working in the church. Mrs. Hicks has been a member of Mount Carmel Methodist Church for 45 years. When she first began attending church there was just a small one room frame building.

During the time she has been a member she has taught Sunday school for several years. She always taught the beginners class.

Mrs. Hicks has been a member of the Woman's Society for Christian Service in the church for about 20 years. During the time she has been a member of this organization she has held every office from president on down.

During the 45 years she has been a member of the church she has worked on many project to improve the church. The latest project was the purchase of carpet for the church which will be laid soon. She aided in getting stained glass windows and the addition of several rooms to the building.

The church that started as a small building has grown into a large sanctuary with several Sunday school class rooms. Each addition to the building as well as everything done in improving it took much work to raise funds. Bake sales, fashion shows, and harvest day sales are just a few of the things that Mrs. Hicks took part in to help raise needed funds.

Mrs. Hicks has been a member of the choir in the church for several years. Just recently she was made a life time member of the Mount Carmel Home Demonstration club. This club was organized about 10 years ago. During the time she has been a member she has held several offices. She is at the present time garden and health leader in the club. In the club she has worked on several projects for the betterment of the community.

Mrs. Hicks spends some of her time around the home working with flowers. In some of the shows in that area and surrounding communities she has come out with top honors. Her favorite flower is the Pink begonia. She has taken honors in several flower shows with this flower. A lot of her flowers are for the church.

Mrs. Frank Hicks has done much to make the Mount Carmel community a better place in which to live, and she always has had a helping hand for those in need. The *News-Argus* is proud to honor her as the Rural Lady of the Week.

Sunday Dinner at Mama Ellen's & Papa Frank's House

As a little girl going to Mama Ellen's and Papa Frank's house for dinner after church with them and Aunt Ava was something I looked forward to all week. I've always had a fear of worms and snakes so just imagine how big my eyes must have been when one Sunday Aunt Ava poured a can of peas into a pan to warm and on top of the peas lay a long crimpy worm. Aunt Ava just spooned the worm out of the pot and into the trash can and we ate the peas for dinner that day. Now 65-70 years later I still think it was hard for me to eat the peas Aunt Ava put on my plate that day. Those Sunday dinners and get-togethers with them would be a treat today.

— *Sandra Hicks Benton*

Papa Frank Loses Mama Ellen

One famous Papa Frank story goes as follows … One Sunday coming home from church Papa Frank, driving an old, worn out, Nash car made the left turn on to Airport Road, probably going a bit too fast. When he made the turn, the door on the passenger side opened and Mama Ellen fell out. Papa Frank continued on his way home. Uncle Casper came along as Mama Ellen was brushing herself off. He took her home. When Mama Ellen got home, Papa Frank says, "Ellen, you could get hurt doing something like that." Mama Ellen went in the house, called Uncle George and told him to bring her a new car the next day. The next day Uncle George arrived with a new Plymouth.

— *As told by Georgia Smith Futrell*

* * * *

There's another family story about Mama Ellen picking cotton all day and then giving birth to a baby boy that night. Uncle George was the only boy who could fit the story with a birthday of November 21, 1920.

Tavie Frank Hicks

Mary Ellen Scott Hicks

* * * *

Papa Frank was known to be a character by all who knew him. He was also known to be hard-headed and stubborn and very set in his ways, especially in his later years.

My two favorite stories I heard many times are as follows.

Papa Frank always went to Pikeville every afternoon. Even when his eyesight was failing, he insisted on continuing his daily routine. Unfortunately, I can't remember names, but one afternoon he ran off the road and ran over someone's mailbox on the way to Pikeville. Of course, he didn't stop. But the incident was seen by a neighbor, so pretty soon the word was out. When asked about the incident, he stated "He (the owner of the mailbox) shouldn't have had his mailbox so close to the road."

On another afternoon, while in Pikeville on his daily trip, he hit someone's car near Uncle Milton's drugstore. Of course there were witnesses. When asked about this incident Papa Frank simply stated "He (the man who's car he hit) shouldn't have been in town the same time I was."

I was very young, but I do have some memories of Christmas Day at Papa Frank and Mama Ellen's house, everyone getting together and playing outside with all my cousins! When I went back years later, the dining room was not nearly as large as I had remembered.

The big, it seemed to me, back porch with the tall steps going outside is another memory I enjoy. Aunt Ava told the story of her youth when Papa Frank and the boys went to the coast fishing. They would come back and dump a bucket of crabs on the back porch and they were all scared of them. At that time, they didn't know they could eat them and how good they would be.

Visiting this house was just so different from anything else I experienced growing up and I always looked forward to a visit.

— Frank B. Powell, III

Papa Frank and Mama Ellen at their 50th Anniversary party in the dining room of their house.

Papa Frank and Mama Ellen at their house in 1966.

Inez Isadora Hicks

Inez Isadora Hicks

The first of eight children, Inez Isadora Hicks was born on November 20, 1906, in the first house Frank and Mary Ellen lived in. She married David Leo Smith December 24, 1928. They had three children; Sarah, 1931; Jane, 1937 and Georgia, 1944. The also had two sons who died at birth and a twin to Georgia, Judy Ava who also died at birth.

Inez was a homemaker all her life. She raised three daughters, Sarah, Jane and Georgia, She was very active in church, teaching the smallest children in Sunday school in the Card Class ages 4, 5 and 6. She always had a pretty garden. She was a great baker specializing in cakes, little pies, and apple jacks which she sold at the Curb Market in downtown Goldsboro. About 10 or 12 ladies gathered every Friday to sell baked goods, chicken salad, cooked vegetables, fresh produce and fruits from their garden. Also butter, milk, pecans and anything extra which they had on hand.

Inez enjoyed playing the piano and singing. She raised chickens and had a cow to milk twice a day. She was a great seamstress making her clothes and her daughters' clothes, especially a new Easter dress for each daughter every year. Her last seven years she was dietitian in the lunchroom at Charles B. Aycock High School in Pikeville. Inez was always busy doing something.

— *Georgia Allen Smith Futrell*

* * * *

I remember Aunt Inez being a great cook. Her desserts were wonderful.

My senior year in high school she worked in the cafeteria and she put her special touch on everything. It was also nice to see her smile everyday.

— *Branda Hicks Lane*

* * * *

 Everyone remembers Aunt Inez for her wonderful cooking and her sweet disposition. On one trip "down home" (that's what we called going to Pikeville for a visit), we stopped at Charles B. Aycock High School where Aunt Inez worked in the school cafeteria. Just when we got there, she was taking a huge pan of homemade yeast rolls out of the oven. She promptly gave us all one with a wad of butter melting inside. That made quite an impression on me and I can still see that big pan of rolls!

— Carolyn Jean Powell

* * * *

 I always remember Aunt Inez for being so nice to me whenever I was around her. And yes, I do remember those rolls! We usually saw her whenever we went "down home" for a visit.

 She was the only person I knew who sold her house, had it moved away, and then built a new house on the same spot. Once Papa Frank passed away, Mama Ellen lived with her and Georgia at the new house which we visited often.

 Carolyn and I spent the weekend with them when Alan Scott and Cindy got married in Virginia. We had a good time, and yes, we had rolls!

— Frank B. Powell, III

* * * *

 Aunt Ava was a tomboy and Aunt Inez was not. They were all in the yard one day, boys and girls. Ava had done something, I don't remember what. Mama Ellen came out of the house and Aunt Ava told Aunt Inez to watch this, "I'm going to pass out." Sure enough she did, but it didn't make any difference. Mama Ellen lit into her with a switch and she came to real quick.

— Ray Hicks

Georgia and Aunt Inez on Christmas Day, 1971.

Allen Milton Hicks

Allen Milton Hicks

The second of eight children, Allen Milton Hicks was born on March 3, 1908. He married Mabel Christine Lee on September 15, 1940. They had three children; Diane, 1945; Allen, 1948; and Lisa, 1961.

The 1st memory I have that stands out is about 3 ½, (Summer 1945) a picnic near Chimney Rock. I fell in and was told that Aunt Ava ran over the rocks and pulled me out by my hair. I remember being under water and seeing bright lights. I almost drowned that day.

(December 25, 1946) Right after the war, we were living in Charlotte. We had a new car and Dad, Mother and I were on our way to Mama Ellen's and Papa Frank's for Christmas Day. As we came into Smithfield, we had a head on wreck with a man in a big truck, but it was not the guy's fault. With us barely not getting killed, Mama and Daddy were in the hospital. I remember Aunt Ava rocking me in a rocking chair there.

We went back to Charlotte and Mama had Allen on November 8, 1947. Dad took a job in Greenville, South Carolina, and we were there, until he decided to go to Kinston to work for Stanley Drug Store. Dad found out the owner was involved in selling drugs and decided to leave.

Papa Frank told Dad about the Drug Store in Pikeville, and that it was up for sale. Papa Frank loaned Dad $2,000 to make a down payment. Dr. Pate came about the same time. Dr. Rose was a doctor living in Pikeville, and he was very happy and content on the farm, with the cows and didn't keep regular office hours. Dr. Pate did the business of three doctors "according to Dad." He even went on call at night, helping Dr. Pate with babies and such. They were good friends until death separated them.

Dad took so much pride in helping the people in the community of Pikeville. Needless to say, he would open the store three or four times on a Sunday, and that was even after store hours. Dad worked a good business, but he never paid himself a salary. When he retired, he had very little to live on.

(1957) Big event in our lives was the day we moved to our house in Pikeville. We had first lived in a four-room log cabin on Mt. Carmel Road. It was near what is now called Airport Road. We had no running water, no bathroom either. Those were some of our most happy times though. There were times Dad had been better, but he had a hard time with ulcers. Mother said it was some of her happiest years in that house. Allen ran like a wild Indian all over the place, many stories to tell during that period.

We lived in a log cabin until Aunt Doris and Uncle Otto moved to their new house. So we moved to live next door to Mama Ellen, Papa Frank, Casper and the rest of the family.

There was still no running water or a bathroom. Dad gave Mama both, Ha Ha! The bathroom was on a slant floor, and you could go through the back window to get to the bathroom. I loved the tin roof when it rained and the sound it made. I could go on forever telling stories about that time.

One memory that stands out to me is when we went over to Uncle Otto's, when there was a hurricane, because they had a new brick house. While we were there the top blew off the tobacco barn and it blew the window in at Uncle Otto's. Uncle Casper lost his roof, but the only damage we had was the swing set that had been blown over by the storm.

Mother and Dad having Lisa made my life complete. When Lisa was three months old, I left for college. Everyone had pictures of their boyfriends, and I had a few 11 x 20 pictures of Lisa. We have a very special relationship till this day and always will. It is so strong. Losing Allen was so hard, for the both of us, for everyone. We celebrated his life this week. He has been gone for 10 years.

— *Diane Blake April 23, 2016*

Rest In Peace Allen Hicks
November 8, 1947-April 20, 2006

My earliest memory at Mama Ellen and Papa Franks was running around that big yard and porch. Her cooking me eggs and drinking that delicious scuppernong juice in a mason jar. Their freezer was always full of some type of ice cream or sweets. Papa Frank would only let me have one of his peppermint bon-bons when he shared them with me. And I believe he hated my name because he would ask my parents "why would you name the girl Litha?"

I spent more time with Uncle Walton and Aunt Ava, with them living next door. We gathered there for crab soup and Thanksgiving on occasions. That's when my cousins would play games, and pull out that one box of toys that have to be 80 years old now. Hey, where are those toys? It was a place for gathering more than any other home after Ma Ellen and Pa Frank passed. The Aycocks also had a home on the coast and I saw Aunt Mary Ellen and her family there.

I remember being on that breezeway listening and watching traffic and praying for a breeze! My first try with alcohol was there when I was around 5 or 6. Aunt Ava made wine and put it in a big Coke bottle in the fridge. Well, being 5 years old, I thought it was Coke. It looked like Coke and it was sweet. They all realized late in the afternoon why I was acting so strange when they found an almost empty Coke bottle. Mama said I was giggling and running around almost hysterically. They said I eventually passed out.

My next drinking episode happened while fishing with dad in the sound on his boat. I guess they didn't have bottled water back then, so when I complained how thirsty I was Dad pulled out a mini County Club for me.

I would like to have more memories of the Hicks family episodes like Diane and Allen, but I came along mighty late in life to this family. I learned more in my 20s and 30s from all the storytelling that my immediate family shared and then from aunts, uncles and cousins. Like many families, ours is one rich in history and heritage and we are who we are because of that. I was so blessed to be in this family and only regret not having more memories of the "old" days with all the cousins.

I have good thoughts about Diane and Allen and wanting to be everywhere they were. Diane entertained me with music, dancing, movies and funny stories. I followed Allen around like a puppy and lost soul wanting to do everything he did. We did some crazy things together that Mom would not approve of! Such as driving in his sports car more than 100 miles an hour, flying with him and he telling me I had to take over.

Also, I had good times with Dad and Walton playing golf. I saw how grown men went to the bathroom ... 1 and 2 on the course. I heard a bunch of cussing out there as well. Especially when I almost turned Walt and me over on the cart. I could go on and on about my Mom, Dad, sister and brother but that's another book.

I am hoping that we can continue getting together and passing on more memories to our other cousins and family.

— Lisa Hicks Hooks, April 23, 2016

* * * *

I remember going shopping in Raleigh with my mother, Aunt Ava, Aunt Lib, and Aunt Mabel. This was in the 1950s. They would dress up for shopping and lunch. They wore a suit or dress, a hat, heels and white gloves. I thought they were elegant and beautiful. The shopping was serious and was an all day event.

— Branda Hicks Lane

* * * *

Uncle Milton's drug store had lots of magazines and comic books. Whenever he restocked, he had to tear half of the front covers off and dispose of them. He would take all of the comics,etc to the farm and dump them in the woods. Ray, Frank and I would go and take as many comics as we could carry. It was a kid's treasure trove and I became an avid reader.

— Branda Hicks Lane

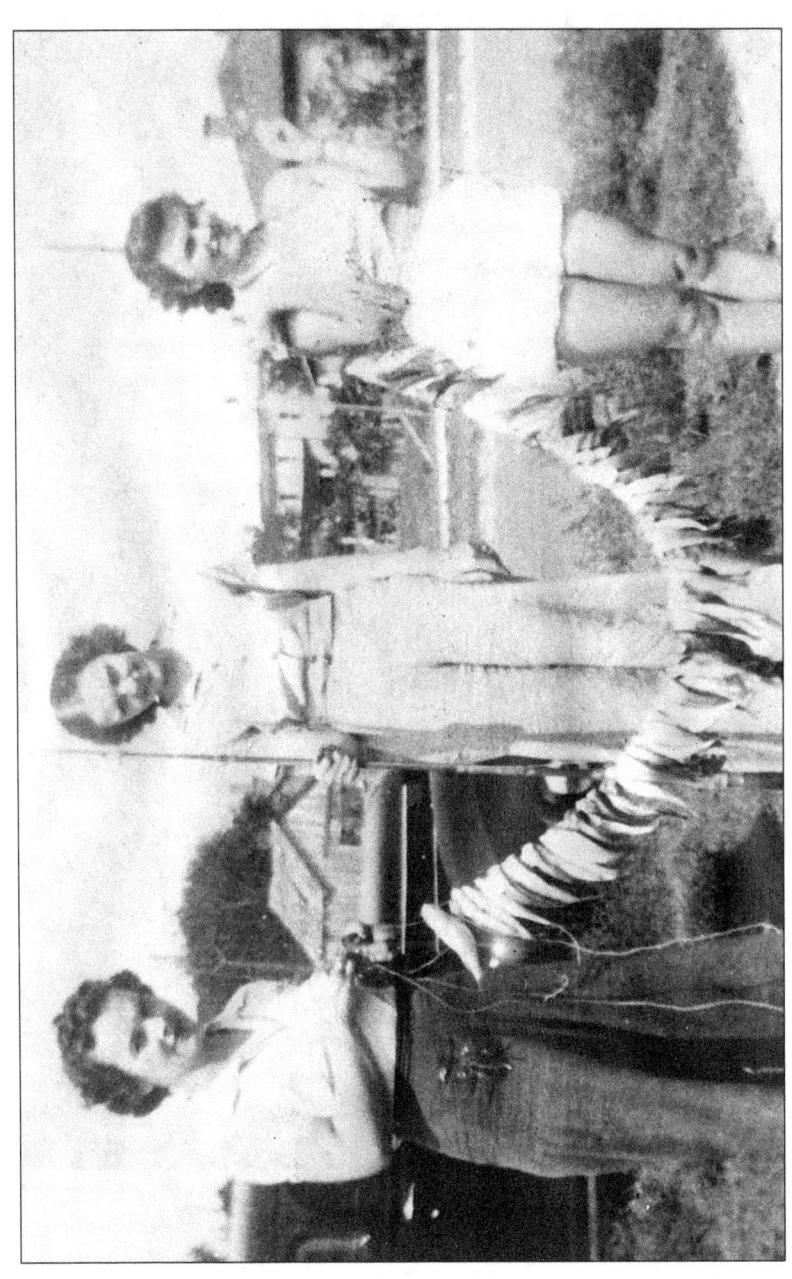

Ava, Mabel and Mary Ellen at a campground near Morehead City, NC, with a day's catch.

John Andrew and Mary Hicks

John Andrew Hicks

The third of eight children, John Andrew Hicks was born on April 7, 1909. He married Mary Noble Sasser on November 29, 1933. They had three children; Janet, 1936; Sandra, 1938; and Johnnie, 1951.

John Hicks of Pikeville Emphasizes Beef Production

This is the first in a series of articles on Wayne's "Farmer of the Week." These progressive farmers, aside from carrying out a diversified farm program, also take advantage of the latest agricultural practices and are actively interested in their community's progress.

One of the best examples in what agricultural specialist call "balanced farming" is found on 150-odd acres owned and operated by John Hicks of Pikeville.

Slim, black-haired, 42-year-old Hicks — who looks 32 — has made a successful farm operation not only out of tobacco, cotton and other row crops, but also beef cattle production and forestry.

His farm is about one mile from Pikeville and is split by the Wilson highway. When he first started farming on his own back in 1934, Hicks didn't have one acre of land under his own name. Now, besides the Pikeville operation, he owns a tenant-operated, 102 acre farm in Brogden.

Hicks says he made good by "workin', savin' and being lucky enough to get the right set-up." A good 50 acres of the Pikeville farm is made up of healthy well-maintained stands of loblolly pine. "They're slow in payin'off," states Hicks, "But they're a lot better than idle land."

For the past several years, the successful farmer has been emphasizing beef cattle production. He's been selling some 15-18 head each year.

"I didn't make any money the first year I started with beef. But I've been doing all right ever since," he says.

Hicks plans to level off selling 20 head yearly. His foundation herd is made up of pure-bred guernseys. And for pasture, he "sows only the best" — landio clover and fescue.

Luckily Hicks has had little trouble with disease affecting his money crop. "Last year," he says "my tobacco crop was the best I've ever had." The tobacco variety he uses has his own name — "Hicks."

The farmer realizes he took something of a chance by using a non-resistant variety with black shank, Granville wilt and root knot so bad in Wayne last year. But he prefers Hicks for its "good quality and good yield."

However, he did plant a little Dixie Bright in 1951, found it did "pretty well." This season he's trying some 181 to see which of the two varieties he likes the best. But he's still sticking with Hicks primarily.

He apportions cotton, corn, vegetables and some fruit among the rest of his acreage.

Hicks and his wife, Mary, have a six-room house conveniently located just off the Wilson highway.

To fill it they have three children, two of whom attend school — Janet, 15, a member of the Future Homemakers of America; and Sandra 13.

And their third is seven-year-old Johnnie, a girl (Hicks says he and his missus were pretty sure Johnnie was going to be a boy. But the stork had different news for them. They gave the child a boy's name anyway).

Aside from being practical enough to carry out a program of balance farming, Hicks also takes advantage of the latest farm practices, brought through the state Extension Service, and is interested in his community's affairs.

He also shows a knowledge of good economics. For he says he won't expand his acreage for the present, but "just hold tight" until inflation is over.

* * * *

I loved spending the night at Uncle John and Aunt Mary's house. Sandra and Janet would tolerate having a younger cousin around. Janet would let me ride with her cruising Center Street on the weekend. Center Street was where all the action was in the 1950s. Another perk was Uncle John cooking a big country breakfast. He was a good cook.

— *Branda Hicks Lane*

FARMER OF THE WEEK JOHN HICKS, Pikeville, stands beside on of the purebred Guernseys he uses for beef production on his 150 acre farm off the Wilson highway. Beef raising is important in versatile Hicks farm program as he sells about 18 head yearly. Aside from his tobacco and cotton crops, Hicks has some 50 acres devoted to loblolly pine, background.
(*News Argus* Photo)

Ava Frances Hicks

Ava Frances Hicks

The fourth of eight children, Ava Frances Hicks was born on September 20, 1911. She married Walton Alex Aycock on January 20, 1936. They had no children.

Memories of Ava and Walton Aycock

My earliest recollections are of their home in rural Wayne County. In the beginning, there was actually an outhouse behind the residence, but this was later replaced with indoor plumbing. Aunt Ava had her ubiquitous gaggle of plants of all kind, particularly including iris and pomegranate. There was a large garden to the left of the house as one faced it from the road, where there was every kind of vegetable imaginable: butter beans, snap beans, corn, tomatoes, bell peppers and okra.

I seem to remember a shed or barn across the road, where there was a tractor that Uncle Walton would use in tilling land nearby, and when he was doing so, Ava would sometimes bring lunch to him in the field. On occasion, he was known to ride the tractor sans both shirt and pants.

The summers that I spent there involved working in the garden, picking blackberries at an Aycock family property down the road, homemade ice cream, frozen SunDrops, and Coca-Colas in 6 ½ ounce bottles with salted peanuts poured in the neck. There were lunches of meat and vegetables, followed by soap operas and a nap on the couch. I sometimes accompanied Walton when he was grafting pecan seedlings, and he taught me how to use a knife with parallel double blades to cut a strip from one variety and graft it onto another.

The front door of that house led directly into what functioned as a den. There was no foyer, and directly adjacent to that room was a more formal living room, where the television resided, and where I watched endless episodes of *Gunsmoke* and *Have Gun Will Travel*. I also recall seeing bits and pieces of the 1957 college national championship game there, in which UNC defeated Kansas and Wilt Chamberlain in triple overtime.

There were frequent bridge games in that front room, usually involving my parents, Mary Ellen and Frank Powell and Ava and Walton. That room led into a kitchen and dining area, where there was a black rotary dial phone, connected to a party line shared with several nearby houses. One never knew when picking up the phone to make a call whether someone else would already be using it.

Ava and Walton's bedroom was off the kitchen, and beyond that was eventually a full bath, that connected on the other side to another bedroom where I usually slept. On one occasion, a traveling encyclopedia salesman visited. He stayed several hours, even being invited to lunch, and Walton eventually bragged on my academic prowess to the point that he had no choice but to buy the books.

I was privileged to travel with them as well. One particular trip to the Cherokee Indian reservation stands out. They bought a pair of moccasins for me and a small Indian drum. Ava and Walton told me years later that as I was having my picture taken with a native in full headdress, I asked when we were going to see a real Indian. Often when we traveled, whether just to Goldsboro or farther away, Walton would buy me a banana split, just to watch me eat it.

When they moved to the new brick house in Pikeville next to Milton and Mabel, I was older and spending less time with them. However, my memories of Ava's Japanese garden and the jungle that the yard eventually became are vivid. I would still spend time there, even in high school when there were many other things vying for my attention. There were golf outings with Walton, to Goldsboro or Wilson, as well as trips to their house on Gale's Creek in Carteret County. An image which remains indelible, and likely in no small measure influenced the role church plays in my life today, is of Ava, on Saturday evening, curling upon the couch in her pajamas and reviewing the material for the Sunday School class she would lead at Mt. Carmel the following day. Recording these recollections brings back a flood of pleasant memories and reminds me of the important role that Ava and Walton played in my childhood, and thus in the adult I became. I can only hope that I have had such a positive influence on the lives of my children.

— *Alan Scott Hicks*

Ava and Walton Aycock

Aunt Ava and Uncle Walton

Most of my memories of Aunt Ava and Uncle Walter center on the house in Pikeville, beside Uncle Milton and Aunt Mabel and the cottage at Gales Creek and later Broad Creek.

After Daddy died in 1966, we spent a lot of time with Aunt Ava and Uncle Walton. In fact, the house in Pikeville was just a familiar and welcoming to me as my home in Henderson. I can still feel the warmth of entering into the house through the breezeway, after what to me was a long trip from Henderson, to be greeted by a big hug from Aunt Ava and the delicious smells of supper. Later Uncle Walton would arrive and there would be another big hug!

I can't think about Aunt Ava without thinking about all of the yummy food: turkeys and hams at Thanksgiving and Christmas, Brunswick stew, homemade wines fermenting in the utility room, family gatherings at Thanksgiving and Christmas after Mama Ellen and Papa Frank were no longer able to host. At Gales Creek, there were crab stews and freshly caught fried fish with slaw, hash browns and hushpuppies. Aunt Ava introduced me to hummingbird cake, still a favorite, when the recipe appeared in *Southern Living* magazine for the first time in the late 70s. And of course, everyone's favorite, Apple Dumplings.

Not only was there food, but the flowers. For as long as I can remember, Aunt Ava provided flowers for Mt. Carmel UMC, every Sunday, and always from her yard. No store bought flowers for her! On the rare occasions someone else wanted to put flowers in the church in memory or honor of someone, she would actually be insulted and would criticize the arrangement throughout the service. You could never go anywhere until the flowers were "fixed" for the church. I have spent many an hour sitting at the bar watching her create arrangements, sometime from nothing at all.

Aunt Ava & Uncle Walton often hosted the garden club meetings, especially when the Japanese garden and yard were in full bloom. The yard and garden put on quite a show! She decorated the Charles B. Aycock birthplace at Christmas, for years as well as extensive Christmas decorations in their Pikeville home. Aunt Ava won many awards for her flower arranging at the local and state levels. She was invited to decorate the NC Governor's Mansion on two different occasions.

I also remember the 1966 white Plymouth station wagon with the red vinyl interior and no AC. You "cooled off" by rolling down the windows and opening vents in the front seat. That car took me to the beach for the first time, to my first baseball game, to my first trip to the mountains and countless other adventures and road trips.

One particular memory with Aunt Ava occurred during Thanksgiving. After a large lunch, Frank, Beth Pate, Aunt Ava and I were walking behind the house. Suddenly, bullets starting flying over our heads! Aunt Ava said "Hit the ground" and we all dropped to our bellies. When the shooting stopped, Aunt Ava looked at us all and said "Run like hell" and we all headed for the house. We later found out that Allen Milton was practicing his shooting.

Uncle Walton was just as a significant figure in my life as Aunt Ava. I always think of him and his pecan trees, Red Man chewing tobacco and a nice highball. He was the breakfast cook. I remember waking up to the smells of bacon, sausage or country ham accompanied by thick hotcakes or cheese drop biscuits. After Thanksgiving or Christmas there was often turkey hash and sometime salted mullets, fried so crisp you could eat the bones, dipped in molasses.

There were fishing trips with Uncle Walton and Uncle Milton. The house on Gales Creek was surround on three sides by water and to this day, I do not understand why we had to get up before the sun came up, get in the car pulling the boat, and drive someplace to "put the boat in" to fish. Often at Gales Creek, Uncle Walton would get up early, wake up everyone, go down to the bridge to fish. He would return, sometimes with fish, and promptly have a nap.

One significant memory with Uncle Walton was the time he sank his brother's (George Wayne) boat. George Wayne had a house near the Gales Creek house and he had a boat.

Ava and Mary Ellen in the kitchen of Ava and Walton's house in Nahunta, NC.

It was basically a john boat, with a motor, even though it was not set up to have a motor. One afternoon, Uncle Walton decided to take us fishing. Frank, Sara and I get the boat. Before leaving, George Wayne cautioned, several times, not to turn the motor unless it was in the water, otherwise, the motor would cut into the side of the boat. We are out in the inland waterway, in front of the house and a storm began to develop. The sky got dark, the water got choppy and Uncle Walton decided to head for shore. However, the water was so rough that it forced the boat motor up, in the midst of a turn, and cuts a hole in the side of the boat. When we began to take on water, we realized what had happened. We started bailing and limped to the dock at Camp Morehead. I was sent to the office at the camp to make the necessary phone calls for assistance. Was George Wayne steamed!!!! No words spoken, boat wenched up on the trailer and gone. Upon returning to the house, Uncle Walton mixes us all a highball. Aunt Ava questions whether or not he should be giving the "children" liquor (all three of us well over drinking age). Frank says: "Aunt Ava, when you see your life pass before you, you kinda need a drink."

I would often tag along with Uncle Walton and Uncle Milton when they would play golf in Goldsboro. At 80 years old, Uncle Walton made a hole-in-one at the Goldsboro course!

As loving and giving as they both were, they could often be harsh critics of family, friends and the world. I am sure many of us have felt the bite of a comment or attitude from one or both of them.

Aunt Ava died on December 23, 1996, my 39th birthday. Uncle Walton died on December 23, 1997, my 40th birthday.

— Carolyn Jean Powell

Otto Frank Hicks

Otto Frank Hicks

The fifth of eight children, Otto Frank Hicks was born on April 20, 1915. He married Doris Lee Smith on February 22, 1939. They had two children; Branda, 1942 and Phyllis 1948.

My fondest memories as a child centered around the church and a big extended family of grandparents, aunt, uncles, and cousins, who lived nearby. Many in the Hicks family attended the same church. I remember my dad, Otto, saying he started attending church as a newborn and seldom missed a Sunday through the years. Everyone in the Hicks family had a talent to share — singing, playing musical instruments, teaching, arranging flowers, and leadership roles — superintendent, treasurer, secretary. My grandmother and my aunts were my Sunday School teachers. I liked to sit with Aunt Ava during church services because she would give me gum or candy to keep me quiet.

Until I was around nine years old, we lived next door to Papa Frank and Mama Ellen. Uncle Casper and Aunt Geraldine lived across the road. Uncle Milton and Aunt Mabel lived down the road. Their children were our playmates. My sister, Phyllis and I played dress up, rode bikes, played softball in the cow pasture and played Tarzan in the woods with our cousins. We would swing on vines and Ray did a great Tarzan yell. Ray was older so he was our leader. We had great imaginations.

After church I loved to go to my grandparent's house for lunch. We ate at the big table on the screen porch with other family members. Mama Ellen was a good cook. Her sweet potato biscuits and dog bread (corn bread cooked just for the dog) were my favorite things. I always was on good behavior and used good manners so I could go without my parents. After lunch it was hard waiting for Papa Frank to rest, because we knew he would take the grandchildren to the park. He waited patiently for us to swing and play and then he would take us to buy ice cream.

I loved Christmas like any other kid, but it was also my birthday. My family acknowledged my birthday after we opened the Santa gifts. Sometimes my mother, Doris baked a cake or she would buy a doll cake. It was a Barbie-like doll and the cake was the fancy dress with ruffles out of icing. I thought it was beautiful. On Christmas morning Daddy cooked a big breakfast and we had birthday cake. It became a family tradition. Even after I was married, he would come to my house and we cooked breakfast together. My job was to make the biscuits and I would practice for weeks to get it right. My family made me feel special on my birthday even as an adult.

On Christmas everyone went to Mama Ellen and Papa Frank's house for lunch in the dining room. The ladies in the family out did themselves cooking delicious food for us. Mother often made a Lady Baltimore cake. I remember the men using platters as plates. The adults were served first, but there was lots of food for the grandchildren.

There was always a big tree in the living room someone cut from the farm and the aunts decorated it. Aunt Ava made snow out of detergent flakes for the tree. So after lunch we gathered around the tree to exchange gifts. Our grandparents always gave each kid a dollar for Christmas. The amount never increased with inflation.

My dad was an avid reader. My earliest memories were of him reading the newspaper, *Readers Digest, Life Magazine*, and nonfiction books. He read the comics to Phyllis and me when we were little kids. He didn't go to college, but he was a life long learner.

I remember him sitting on a bench at the mall reading a book while Mother and I were shopping. I think his love of books and knowledge influenced me to become a teacher.

Mother and Daddy were always involved with our school and our different interest.

When we were in elementary school, Mother was a grade mother and helped with PTA events. She made sure we had piano lessons. If we practiced the piano, we didn't have to do the dishes. That was a no brainer for me.

I was a cheerleader and Phyllis played basketball and was a majorette in high school. Daddy attended every game. Daddy served on the school board even after we graduated. He cared about education.

— Branda Hicks Lane
April 22, 2016

One of my first memories was at 3-years-old was of Granny Scott dying. I remember lots of family being at Mama Ellen and Papa Frank's. I had seen Granny being cared for by Mama Ellen in what later was her and Papa Frank's room. She always had her eyes closed.

Another dying memory was of Uncle Bud, Mama Ellen's brother, being "laid out" in his coffin is their big living room in front of the windows where the Christmas tree was placed. I was struck by his ruddy complexion and profile of his face in the coffin making him look like an Indian chief.

In the 1990s when they cut the huge, old oak tree down which was located in front of the old pump house at Mama Ellen and Papa Frank's. Daddy and I went over to see the big tree stump. I remember daddy looking so small sitting on the big stump. He told me how he had told Papa Frank he was scared to move to the big house because the wind blowing through the big oak trees frightened him. Daddy said he was three years old when they moved to the big house.

When thinking about my growing up, I realized grandparents, aunts, uncles and lots of cousins were my most significant relationships. It seemed our age differences didn't seem to matter. There were the Tarzan theme play times in the woods with Ray, Frank, Joy, Allen, Diane, Branda and me. The ball games we had in the pasture at Uncle Casper and Aunt Geraldine's. The Christmas lunches at Mama Ellen and Papa Frank's with all 35 of us filling that huge dining room! We all were important receiving our $2.00 from our grandparents every Christmas. When we married, it jumped to $5.00! Then we had the BBQs where the dads stayed up all night cooking the hogs. The Easter Egg Hunts which Uncle Milton recorded on his movie camera! Our trips to Herman Park to ride the train with Papa Frank on Sunday's with whoever could cram in his car. All of this provided the life long value that family is important.

— Childhood Memories of Phyllis Hicks Marsh

* * * *

Uncle Otto always gave me a dry haircut and messed my hair up. He only messed my hair up at church. Extra hair spray didn't slow him down, or boyfriends being at church with me!

— Melody Hicks James

* * * *

Uncle Otto loved baseball. One day he came out of the house in his baseball uniform. I wanted to go see that game real bad. Daddy (Uncle Casper) asked Uncle Ott who his team was playing. Uncle Ott told him and Daddy sort of wanted to see the game also, so he took me. I got to see Uncle Ott catch in that game, and Uncle Ott was good. I knew from that day that I wanted to watch baseball games.

One story told was when there was a baseball diamond at Church, Mount Carmel. There was a big Oak tree down the left field line. Otto Hicks hit one of the longest balls ever hit — it cleared the big old Oak tree. Uncle Otto was a very good ball player.

— Ray Hicks

Otto and Doris Hicks

Ottio and Doris were married on February 22, 1939, at the Minister's Chapel at Duke. Mount Carmel's minister was a divinity student there at this time. It was his suggestion they meet him at Duke.

William Casper Hicks

William Casper Hicks

The sixth of eight children, William Casper Hicks was born on April 3, 1917. He married Geraldine Forehand in October, 1937. They had four children; Ray, 1940; William Frank 1943; Joy, 1950; and James, 1957.

On April 3, 1917, a green eyed baby boy with black hair was born to Frank and Ellen Hicks. He would grow up to be a handsome man who was devoted to his family. He was supposed to be named after one of the Wise Men but because of the unusual name, it came out Casper.

He was a hard working man, he could build anything and repair as well. He was a great traveling companion but the happiest times for him was on his boat. One thing I think a lot of people do not know about my Father is that he wanted to become a doctor but the times dictated another road for him to take.

He was a great baseball player at the position of catcher during his high school days. The love of his life was Geraldine F. Hicks.

— Joy Hicks Williams

* * * *

I loved living across the road from Uncle Casper and Aunt Geraldine. We always played in their yard or pasture. We would run to the house looking for a snack after playing. Aunt Geraldine would make mayo and mustard sandwiches for us. I remember her always being kind and I loved it when she called me "Shug."

— Branda Hicks Lane

* * * *

Papa Frank had a red Nash Rambler that just set in the yard. I wanted that car. Finally, one day, Papa Frank said me and Frank could drive it a little bit. He told Cap (Uncle Casper) to watch us. We went down the dirt road and went all the way to Patetown! We decided we would fool someone.

So, down near where Sandra's house is today we pulled the car over to the side of the ditch at an angle and waited for another car to come by and help us out. When Daddy found out what we did, it was just about as bad as when we hid in the woods and two ladies came by and we threw dirt clogs at them.

— *Ray Hicks*

* * * *

Uncle Casper was one of the hardest working men I knew. I road with him and Uncle John one time to a funeral and the whole way they talked about the crops and fields we passed by. He worked hard even until he was sick. Right before he passed away he called us all together and said "I've learned one thing, money is not everything. Of course, you have to have a little to get by, but that's not what matters." You know he worked hard and made money all his life, but in the end he realized it didn't matter.

— *Rose Hicks*

* * * *

Daddy bought a brand new Dodge truck. He went to the beach and left me home with that brand new Dodge truck. I looked and found the second set of keys. I shouldn't found them. But a bunch of us boys get together and went over to what they called the sand hole on the river where Lanetree is now. Going down that dirt road we got going pretty fast and the truck hit a soft spot in the road and bounced into a Pine tree. I was even afraid to get out and look at it. I asked one of the boys to get out and look. I said "How bad is it hurt?" He replied, "Pretty bad Ray, the fender is gone." We had to jack the fender off the tire to get it out. After that, it drove alright. I drove it home and parked it right where it was. And had to wait for him to home from the beach. When he drove in the yard he saw it right then. He called "Ray come here." I figured I was going to get it. He said, "You know that hog you've been raising?" I said "yes sir." "When you finish raising it you will get just about enough money to pay for that fender." I never got any money from that hog.

— *Ray Hicks*

* * * *

    We had a lot of guineas, several hundred, mostly older guineas. We had so many because they would eat tobacco worms, they were good wormers. Mama Ellen and Papa Frank, Uncle Otto, and Daddy all had guineas. The road was dirt then and occasionally a car would come by and run over a guinea, sometimes two or three. It was my job to get these guineas before anything would happen to them except for being dead. I would take them to Mama Ellen, Mama, or Aunt Doris and they would make guinea stew. And you never tasted anything as good as guinea stew!

— Ray Hicks

* * * *

    Daddy always had plenty of cows, hogs, chickens and before Christmas he would buy at least 40 turkeys. He would raise them and sell them for Thanksgiving and Christmas. One of the big ones we would eat for Christmas at Papa Frank and Mama Ellen's. That was always a great thing about Christmas. Daddy would always give one to Papa Frank to raise. Papa Frank was going to feed those chickens and turkeys. If you had Papa Frank off anywhere, he had to be home in time to feed those chickens. I bet you that turkey weighed 40 pounds we ate that year for Christmas. I run that turkey for 20 minutes that morning trying to catch him so Papa Frank could kill him.

— Ray Hicks

* * * *

    Then we would have a hog killing. Back then nobody went to the grocery store hardly ever. Everything came out of the garden. We ate a lot of hogs. We would probably kill 10 or 12 hogs and have them hanging up. When you did go to the grocery store it was mostly the fathers who went on Saturday nights. You didn't go in with a cart. You told the man what you needed and he would get it for you. And if it was high up, he had a tool to reach it. But, times did begin to change.

— Ray Hicks

George Appells Hicks

George Appells Hicks

The seventh of eight children, George Appells Hicks was born on November 21, 1920. He married Elizabeth Ann Parker on April 12, 1946. They had one child; Alan Scott, 1947.

He grew up with seven siblings on a farm in rural Wayne County. His college education was cut short by World War II, serving four years in the U.S. Army, including a tour of duty in the Pacific Theater.

Upon his return to civilian life, he went in to business of automobile sales, eventually operating a Chrysler-Plymouth dealership in both Fremont and Wilson. During his business career he served as chairman of the Fremont School Board and president of the Fremont Rotary Club.

Professionally, he served on national and state automobile dealer councils. He was an active member of both the Fremont United Methodist Church and First United Methodist Church in Wilson.

George was an avid hunter and fisherman and enjoyed frequent trips to the North Carolina coasts in pursuit of these endeavors. As a young man, he earned the nickname "Bull," perhaps because of his stubbornness or a penchant for forging ahead no matter what the obstacle. He exhibited both such traits throughout his life, a hallmark of which was his love for and devotion to his extended family in Wayne County.

— *Alan Scott Hicks*

* * * *

I have fond memories of Uncle George and Aunt Lib when Dallas and I moved to Wilson in 1978. We developed a real friendship. They included us in their circle of friends. We had great times dancing at the Wilson Country Club. They could really cut a rug on the dance floor.

— *Branda Hicks Lane*

Mary Ellen Hicks

Mary Ellen Hicks

The eighth of eight children, Mary Ellen Hicks was born on September 6, 1922, the only child born in the hospital. She married Frank B. Powell, Jr. on December 28, 1948. They had two children; Frank, III, 1954 and Carolyn, 1957.

I know many of you have special memories of Mama. Maybe it's a field of sunflowers that she would plant each summer. It could be the first time you saw her on her tractor, that is older than me, cutting grass — acres of grass; a little woman on top of a big tractor was quite a sight. Perhaps it is the taste of pecan pie or pickles. Maybe it was her garden, large enough to feed the neighbors, but without it, she was confident that she would starve. I hope you will hold your memories of her close and that they will be as dear to you as ours are.

Did you know she was born on her father's 40th birthday? Mama was the youngest of eight siblings born to Mama Ellen and Papa Frank. As she would tell the story, when her two sisters found out another baby was on the way, they were mad. Aunt Inez and Aunt Ava thought that there were enough children and that Mama Ellen was too old to have another baby. Aunt Inez was adamant that she would not love the new baby because George, the youngest at the time, was such a sweet, rolly pollie baby she was sure no other could take his place. On the day that Mama was born, Aunt Inez and Aunt Ava were so excited they could hardly wait to go in and see the new baby. They were charged with naming their new sister and named her Mary Ellen, after their mother. Born on her father's birthday while he was in Goldsboro selling tobacco; named after her mother.

Mama thrived in Pikeville on the family farm, becoming a star guard on the Pikeville High School basketball team. Because of her small stature, many of her classmates called her "Runt." I attended her 50th high school reunion with her and they were still calling her that. After graduating Pikeville High

School, she was bound for Suffolk, VA, for nursing school. She was such a "runt" her nursing shoes had to be special ordered in a size 2½.

Nursing school in Suffolk, VA led to work in Henderson at Maria Parham Hospital. Mama was a registered nurse and while she had not worked in 57 years, she always told her nurses in the hospital that she was an RN. I think she thought she got better care once they knew that she knew what they should be doing and how they should be doing it. While working at the hospital, she met Daddy on a blind date and after about a five-year courtship, they married in 1948. They lived with Daddy's parents on Garnett Street for five years until they moved to the country.

Now Daddy was really a city boy who fancied himself a farmer. It was Mama who was the real farmer in the family. Someone once asked me what she had in the garden and when I finished the long list of things growing, the person said, that's not a garden, that's farming! We had the first pick your own strawberry farm in the county and our own asparagus bed. Mama was really a country girl.

In July of 1966 our world was turned upside down when Daddy died at 48 years old. Frank was 12 and I was 8 and from that moment on she became both mother and father to us. She modeled a quiet strength and courage. She shepherded us through childhood, our teenage years, college and into adulthood.

After Daddy died, her father, Papa Frank, though she should sell everything and return to Pikeville where her nearly all her family lived. By that point in her life, she had lived here longer than she had lived in Pikeville and this was home. She felt it was her duty to guard and protect Daddy's legacy and that she did. She showed us resilience and determination and defined for us what it meant to be a responsible adult. That is her legacy to us.

So she stayed here, in our little house on Cooper Grove Road until the end.

We should all be so gifted with a life not only long in years, but rich and bountiful in the fruits of our labors.

I feel the following sums up the last year and a half of her life: From 1 Peter, Chapter 5, verse 10:

After you have suffered for a little while, the God of all grace, who has called you to his eternal glory in Christ, will himself restore, support, strengthen and establish you.

Thanks be to God.

— *Carolyn Jean Powell*

* * * *

My favorite memory of Aunt Mary Ellen was when I had my tonsils removed. I remember being very scared. She told me that I could have all the ice cream I wanted after the surgery. Because she was a nurse, she went into surgery with me and stayed with me until I went home. She was the best.

— *Branda Hicks Lane*

* * * *

A story our mother always told us was about when she, our father and his father, who everyone called "Pappy" traveled down to Wayne County to attend a pig picking at Uncle Casper's.

It seems the entire Hicks clan was present for this event and as was the custom of the day, they had invited the preacher, I assume from Mt. Carmel. I can just see the scene — a long table under those big trees beside the house with everyone sitting around.

When it came time to eat Pappy asked my father to get him a beer out of the trunk of the car. My father said "Are you sure? You're sitting beside the preacher." Pappy said "yes, just pour it in a paper cup."

Mama said Daddy did just that and Pappy enjoyed his BBQ with a beer while dining beside the preacher. This happened before I was born so it was sometime between December 1948 and January 1954.

— *Frank B. Powell, III*

Frank B. Powell, Jr. with Janet and Sandra Hicks at the Aycock homeplace near Nahunta, NC.

Recipes

Mabel's Sausage Balls (Diane Hicks Blake)

Mom always made these during the holidays.

1 lb. hot sausage
1 lb. sharp cheddar cheese
3 c. bisquick

Grate cheese, mix with sausage and bisquick. Roll into small balls. Bake on cookie sheets at 350 degrees until brown. Can store in freezer and reheat.

Cut Glass Salad (Diane Hicks Blake)

Set in ice trays:

1 cherry jello (3oz), 1 c. water -(1/2 c. cold)
1 orange jello (3oz), 1 c. water -(1/2 c. cold)
1 lime jello (3oz), 1 c. water -(1/2 c. cold)

After jello has set, use 1 3 oz. package lemon jello, 1/4 c. sugar, 1/2 c. pineapple juice, 1 c. boiling water. Place in refrigerator and set until not quite solid but moves and rolls.

In large bowl, add 2 8 oz. containers of cool whip to lemon mixture and beat with mixer. Cut the jellos into cubes. Fold into cool whip mixture and set for 1 day in 9x13 dish.

Mabel's Saw Dust Salad (Diane Hicks Blake)

Step 1. Dissolve 1 packager lemon and 1 package orange jello in 2 c. boiling water and 1 c. cold water. Set aside to cool. (Use red at Christmas)

Step 2. Mix 1 #2 can crushed pineapple drained (save the juice), 1 small package miniature marshmallows, 3 or 4 sliced bananas. Add all ingredients to the partially set jello.

Pour mixture in a 9x13 dish. Refrigerate until firm.

Step 3. Make a boiled custard by mixing 1 c. pineapple juice, 1 egg, 1/2 c. sugar, 2 heaping T. flour (use double boiler if you have one). Bring to a boil and cook until you have a custard consistency. Cool and spread over the jello mixture in an even layer.

Step 4. Mix 2 packages Dream whip, according to directions (I use cool whip) Mix with 8 oz. cream cheese and 8-10 oz. cheese. Beat until smooth. Spread over custard

Step 5. Grate about 1/4 c. or more of yellow cheese, colby or cheddar, over the top.

Serve over lettuce.

Mabel Lee Hicks Vegetable Beef Soup (Diane Hicks Blake)

1-2 pounds Hamburger
1 onion (chopped)
1 package butterbeans
1 package corn
1/2 package green peas
2 cans green beans
1 can tomato puree
1 can tomato sauce
4-6 potatoes, cubed
1 c. cut up okra
pat of butter

salt and pepper to taste
fresh garlic
parsley
1 T. sugar

Brown hamburger and onions. Add salt and pepper. Add tomatoes plus 5-8 cups water, depending on how rich you like your soup. Bring to boil and start adding beans, corn and peas. Add potatoes last. Cook till tender, not mushy. Add butter to finish. Takes about 50 minutes.

Aunt Ava's Crab Stew (Diane Hicks Blake)

The way I remember Aunt Ava cooking crab stew at the beach house.

Step 1. Pour the live crabs in the sink. Pour boiling water over the crabs. Then clean, making sure you remove the lungs. Then scrub crabs and break in half.

Step 2. In a large pot, place 6 or 7 onion, 2 lb. potatoes cut up 1/4 size, salt, pepper and 1 red pepper. Cover with water, add bacon drippings. Cook until tender. Add the crab meat. In a bowl, mix 1 c. cornmeal, a little salt, 1/4 t. baking powder, cold water to bring together. Form into rounds and flatten out a bit. Put on top of boiling mixture. You may need to add a little water. The dumplings will thicken the stew. Cook until tender. Dish up and give everyone a knife and a nutcracker!

Enjoy!

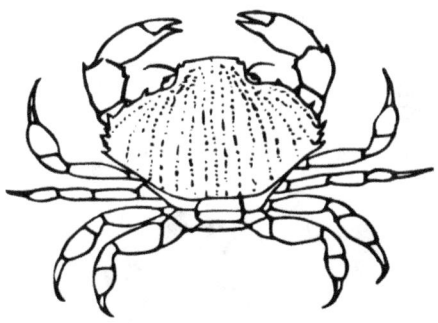

Lisa and Diane's Cream of Crab Soup (Diane Hicks Blake)

2 lb. crab meat
Step 1. Cook 2 chopped onions and 2 stalks celery until tender. Cook 3 or 4 potatoes cut in small blocks. Set aside.
Step 2. Make a white sauce. Use 6 T. butter to 6 T. flour (or more). Add 1 qt. whole milk and 2 c. of half and half, fat free, to mix. Cook. May take a while to thicken. Sometimes we add more flour or milk.
Add parsley, 2 T. dry mustard, dash of worcestershire sauce, hot pepper to taste, Old Bay to taste. Add crab and potatoes. Dish up and enjoy!

Uncle Walton's Fish Stew (Diane Hicks Blake)

I remember going down to their pond. Uncle Walton had a big black wash pot. He used dried corn cobs to make the fire.

Basic, as the crab stew, start with bacon, potatoes and onions, season with salt and pepper. Fish of all kinds can be used. Cook till tender. At the last minute, he would put eggs on the top. He loved that, Aunt Ava didn't. He added the cornmeal dumplings too. He would bring Daddy some, as a couple of times a year the fire department at Nahunta had a fish stew for a fundraiser. Uncle Walton was always active with the cooking.

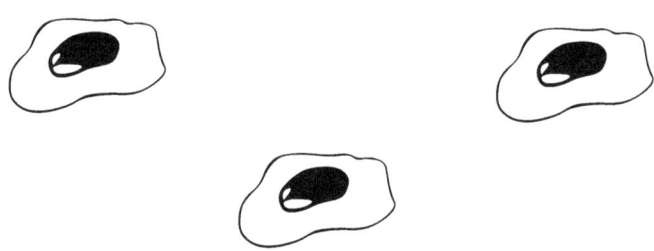

Sarah Smith Pate's Homemade Rolls (Branda Hicks Lane)

3 tsp sugar
3 cups all purpose flour
2 tsp shortening
1 cup buttermilk
1 pkg dry yeast

Sift flour and add sugar and shortening. Mix well and add buttermilk. Dissolve yeast in 1/4 c. lukewarm water and pour into mixture and mix well. Let mixture rest in bowl for two hours. Then take out dough and knead again. Make out about 12 small rolls. Put on greased baking sheet. Let stand another two hours. Cook in 450 degrees oven for 15 to 20 minutes.

This recipe was found in old cookbook published by the Mount Carmel Woman's Society of Christian Service.

Aunt Inez Pastry for pies and tarts (Diane Hicks Blake)

Aunt Inez made tarts every week for the curb market in Goldsboro, along with pastry and chicken salad.

1 3/4 c. crisco
4 c. plain flour
1 t. salt
1 T. sugar
1 egg, beaten
1/2 c. ice water
1 T. vinegar

Cut crisco into flour, sugar and salt with a pastry cutter. Beat egg, vinegar and water. Pour over flour. Knead lightly, store in refrigerator. Pull out as needed. May also freeze.

Mary Ellen's Easy Buttermilk Biscuits

2 c. all purpose flour
2 t. baking powder
1 t. salt
1/4 t. baking soda
1/3 c. Blue Bonnet 53 % vegetable spread
In a large bowl, combine flour, baking powder, salt and baking soda. Cut in spread until mixture is crumbly. Add buttermilk string until mixture forms a soft dough. Place dough on lightly floured surface. Knead lightly 3 or 4 times. Roll out dough to 1/2 inch thickness. With floured 1 3/4 inch cutter, cut out biscuits. Reroll scraps and cut biscuits. Place 1 inch apart on lightly greased baking sheet. Bake at 425 degrees for 12-15 minutes or until golden brown.

Mary Ellen's Blueberry Muffins

1 egg
1/4 c. milk
1/4 c. oil
1 1/2 c. sifted flour
2 t. baking powder
1/2 c. sugar
1/2 t. salt
1 c. blueberries

Mix egg, milk, an oil. Stir in flour and sugar, then berries. Spoon batter into greased or lined muffin tins. Bake at 400 degrees in muffin pan for 15 minutes.

Mary Ellen's Corn Sticks or Cornmeal Muffins

1 c. cornmeal
2 t. baking powder
3/4 t. salt
1 egg
3/4 c. buttermilk
1/2 c. cold water

Beat egg and buttermilk. Add dry ingredients, mixed and sifted together. Add water and beat well. Pour into hot greased muffin pan or corn stick irons. Bake in hot – 450 degrees – oven for about 20 minutes.

Aunt Doris' 16 Day Sweet Pickles (Diane Hicks Blake)

Requires a crock. About 2 gallons of cucumbers (10 pounds); 1 gallon water + 2 cups canning salt. I double this so that would be another gallon water plus 2 cups salt. Cucumbers must be covered with the liquid. Soak for one week. Stir with hands everyday. Cover with glass pie plates to weight down. Remove scum everyday. Cucumbers will change in color.

Day 7. Pour off salt water. Wash good. Wash crock. To each gallon of water add 2 T. alum. Bring to boil and pour over cucumbers. Do this 8th day again.

Day 9. Pour away alum water. Cut the cucumbers in cubes. Place back in crock.

Mix 6 c. sugar, 5 c. dark vinegar, 1 small container pickling spices in cheese cloth (I double this). Bring to a boil and pour over pickles.

For day 10, 11 and 12, each day, add 1 cup sugar to mix and boil (if double add 2 c.)

For day 13, 14, 15 just pour mixture in pan and bring to boil.

Day 16. Place pickles in jar. Process one at a time. Seal.

Ava Aycock's Frozen Pickles (Diane Hicks Blake)

Day 1. 2 c. sugar, 1 T. salt, 1 c. vinegar, 6 c. sliced cucumbers, 1 c. sliced onion, 1 c. sliced peppers.

Mix sugar, salt and vinegar. Pour over vegetables. Let stand overnight in refrigerator.
Day 2. Pour in jars and freeze.

I remember her adding other vegetables. She put up whatever Uncle Walton brought home from the garden.

Diane's Chow Chow (Diane Hicks Blake)

My Aunt Noma made this for us every fall. Now I make it with my daughter Susan. Hope she will continue after me.

12 large peppers (red and yellow)
12 large green tomatoes
6 large onions
1 large head cabbage
2 pods hot pepper

4 c. sugar (you may add extra cup of sugar)
6 c. dark vinegar
3 T. Salt
3 T. pickling spice (tied up in cheese cloth)

Grind all the vegetables. Place in large bowl. Bring sugar and vinegar mixture to boil. Add spice bag. Let boil couple of minutes. Add vegetables. Bring back to boil. Place mix in clean hot jars one at a time. Seal. Have lids in boiling water. Do one at a time.

Mary Ellen's Cinnamon Cucumber Rings

2 gallon sliced cucumber rings
2 c. lime
8 1/2 quarts water
2 c. vinegar
1 T. alum
Red food coloring
2 c. water
10 c. sugar
8 cinnamon sticks
1 c. red hots (make sure red hots do not have starch)

Peel cucumbers, slice and remove seeds. May use large cukes that are turning yellow. Slice about 1/4 inch thick. When sliced and seeded, it will look like a doughnut. Combine sliced rings, lime and water. Soak 24 hours. Drain and wash well. Cover with cold water and soak 3 hours. Return to pot and add 1 cup vinegar, 1 T. alum and 3 T. red food coloring. Add enough water to cover cukes. Put on stove and simmer 2 hours. Drain off and throw away water. Heat and pour over cukes 2 cups vinegar, 2 c. water, 10 c. sugar (or more), 8 cinnamon sticks and 1 c. red hots. Next morning, drain and reheat juice (do not boil). Pour over cukes. Keep lid over cukes to hold steam. Third morning, reheat juice and cukes with cinnamon sticks. Put in jars and seal.

Mama Lee's Bread and Butter Pickles (Diane Hicks Blake)

1 gallon young cucumbers, sliced thin
8 small onions, sliced thin
2 medium bell peppers, sliced (red or yellow)

Place mixture in a large container or a clean kitchen sink. Sprinkle with 1/2 c. canning salt. Mix with hands. Cover with crushed ice. Allow to stand 2 1/2 to 3 hours. Drain in a colander.

Make a mixture of 5 c. dark vinegar, 4 c. sugar, 1 1/2 t. turmeric, 1 1/2 t. ground cloves, 3 t. celery seed, 3 T. mustard seeds.

Bring to a boil. Add cucumbers and heat. DO NOT BOIL. Place in hot jars with hot lids.
Best to place in refrigerator before serving.

Spinach Casserole (or Potato Casserole) Diane Hicks Blake

3 packages frozen chopped spinach
3 T. butter
1 onion
3 T. flour
1 t. salt
1/4 t. pepper
2 c. milk
1/2 c. cheddar cheese

Cook and drain spinach. Set aside. Cook onion in butter until tender, add flour, salt, pepper as mixture browns. Add slowly milk and cheese. Pour mixture over spinach in a 9x13 dish. Top with extra cheese. Bake 350 degrees for 30 minutes.

Diane usually doubles this as everyone loves it! For a potato casserole, cook potatoes and onions. Make the same sauce.

Aunt Ava's Chicken Pastry (Diane Hicks Blake)

Aunt Ava showed me how to make when she and Uncle Walton came to Maryland 44 years ago. Always turns out, a very tender pastry.

Step 1. Have your chicken cooked and picked. You need a large pot with 3 or 4 quarts of liquid. Season broth with salt, pepper and a little butter.

Step 2. In a bowl use about 3 cups of self rising flour, 1 t. salt, 1 large T. crisco. Take about 1/2 to a cup of HOT broth an pour over flour.

Step 3. Stir and form a ball, using more flour if needed. It will be soft or liquid.

Step 4. Roll out, as thin as possible. Cut into strips.

Step 5. In the boiling liquid, turn pot to medium, and start dropping the strips in. Try not to stir, just move around. Once all strips are in cover and turn to low. Cook until tender. Liquid will thicken. 20 to 30 minutes. Add chicken back in. Sometimes you have to add more broth or liquid.

Sweet and Sour Pork (Diane Hicks Blake)

1/2 c. soy sauce
1/2 t. ground ginger
1 garlic clove
2 lb. cubed pork
1/2 to 3/4 c. cornstarch

Soak meat in mixture for about 10 minutes.
Drain, coat in cornstarch and fry in deep fat. Set aside.
Mix and cook together 1 c. pineapple juice, 1/2 c. dark vinegar, 1/4 c. ketchup, 3/4 c. brown sugar, 1 T. worcestershire sauce. Add red bell pepper, onions and pineapple chunks. Add fried pork. Serve over rice.

Doris Hicks' Spaghetti Sauce (Phyllis Hicks Marsh)

2 pound ground beef
2 large onions chopped
1 teaspoon garlic salt
2 cans mushroom
2 cans tomato paste
2 cans tomato sauce
3 cans water, use sauce cans
Salt, Pepper, Celery and bell peppers can be added.

Brown beef,onions,celery and bell peppers. Add mushrooms,tomato sauce, tomato paste water, salt, pepper and garlic salt. Bring to boil and cook on low two hours with lid on pot.

Mom made some of the best spaghetti sauce and she got this recipe from one of her dearest friends Dot Garris. I can remember mom cooking this sauce and the house smelling so good. When I cook spaghetti sauce today, those memories come back and I enjoy the fragrant smells of the cooking sauce as much as eating it. I use to snitch secret tastes of the cooking sauce but mom never caught me!

Maryland Crab Cakes (Diane Hicks Blake)

1 lb. crab meat (or fish)
4 slices white bread crumbs
1 egg
1 T. worcestershire sauce
3 or 4 T. Mayo
1/2 lemon
1/2 t. to 1 T. Old Bay

Mix together and form cake; fry in oil.

Mary Ellen's Sweet Potato Casserole

3 c. mashed sweet potato (baked or boiled)
1 c. sugar
2 eggs
1 t. vanilla
2 T. melted butter
1/2 c. milk

Mix all ingredients well and pour into well greased 2 quart casserole dish. Bake at 350 degrees for 15-20 minutes or until bubbly. Then put on topping.

Topping:
1 c. light brown sugar
1/3 c. self rising flour
2 T. melted butter
1 c. chopped nuts

Mix topping ingredients until crumbly, Crumble over potatoes.

Mama Ellen's Sweet Potato Pudding

3 average size sweet potatoes
1/2 cup milk1/2 cup sugar
3 Tbsp. butter, melted
3 Tbsp. flour
Dash of salt
1 tsp. spice

Peel and grate potatoes. Add sugar, flour, spice, milk, salt and butter. Mix well and pour into a well greased pan. Bake 1/2 hour in 400 degree oven.

Mama Ellen's Loaf Bread Pudding

1/2 cup sugar
Pinch of salt
3 pieces of loaf bread
2 eggs
3 Tbsp. butter
1 tsp. vanilla
1/2 cup coconut

Cut bread into small pieces. Add milk and stir well. Add sugar and well beaten eggs, salt, butter (melted) and vanilla. Add coconut and pour into well greased pan. Bake 1/2 hour in 350 degree oven.

Sandra Benton's Bread Pudding

2 eggs
1 cup sugar
1 1/2 cup milk
5 slices loaf bread cut into small pieces
1/2 tsp. vanilla
2 Tbsp. butter (melted)
1 cup frozen coconut
1/2 cup raisins (optional)

Melt butter in 8" x 8" baking dish. Mix all ingredients together and beat thoroughly. Pour extra butter from baking dish into mixture and mix in. Pour into baking dish. Bake at 375 degrees 40-45 minutes until set and lightly browned.

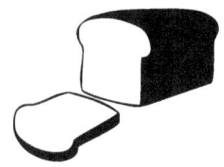

Doris Hicks' Barbecue Chicken Sauce (Phyllis Hicks Marsh)

1 can tomato sauce
1 chopped onion browned in a little butter or fat
2 tablespoons prepared mustard
1 tablespoons Worcestershire
1 tablespoon vinegar
2 tablespoons brown sugar
Little waterBaste chicken.

No other instructions given. It was amazing to go through Mom's old recipes and find this one. I had used an almost identical one for many years. Mine is below. 6-8 chicken pieces

3 tablespoons Worcestershire sauce
1/3 cup oil
2 tablespoons prepared mustard
Small can tomato sauce
2 teaspoons salt
1/2 cup vinegar
1/2 teaspoon black pepper
3 tablespoons sugar

Mix all ingredients and pour over chicken pieces which have been placed in large frying pan. Cover with sauce and cook over low heat until cooked thoroughly. Can cook in oven putting in baking dish at 325 degrees until cooked thoroughly.
— *Phyllis Hicks Marsh*

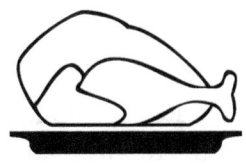

Brunswick Stew Mrs. Walton Aycock

1 chicken
4 pints Irish potatoes (cut in cubes)
4 lbs. beef
4 pints onions
4 lbs. pork
4 quarts tomatoes
4 pints butter beans
1 cup catsup
4 pints garden peas
1 bell hot pepper
4 pints corn
Salt and Pepper to taste

Cook meats till tender. Cut in small pieces, add butter beans, garden peas, then cook five minutes. Add corn, potatoes, tomatoes and catsup. Add hot pepper. Cook until thick (about one hour.)

Meatloaf Sandra Benton

3 lbs ground 85% beef
1 1/2 cups tomato juice
1 cup Irish potatoes (boiled and mashed with fork into small pieces)
1/4 cup catsup
1/2 tsp black pepper
1 1/3 pkgs onion soup mix
12 Zesta crackers, crushed.

Mix all ingredients together and shape into oblong roll and place into casserole dish. Bake at 350 degrees for 1 to 1 1/4 hours. After about 45 minutes of baking pour off any grease that has accumulated in the top with additional ketchup.
(This dish is always requested at Mt. Carmel Church's potluck suppers.)

Lemon Chess Pie (Diane Hicks Blake)

3 eggs
1 1/2 c. sugar
3/4 c. melted butter
1 t. dark vinegar
Juice of 1 lemon

Beat well. Pour into uncooked 9" pie shell. Bake at 325-350 degrees until set and golden. May have to place foil over crust to keep from burning.

Aunt Ava's Buttermilk Pie

2 c. buttermilk
1 c. Sugar
2 T. flour
1/2 t. soda
1 egg

Beat egg and add buttermilk, sugar, flour and soda. Beat until smooth. Pour into unbaked pastry shell. Sprinkle with nutmeg. Bake for 30 minutes at 400 degrees.

Rhubarb Cream Pie (Diane Hicks Blake)

1 c. sugar
2 beaten eggs
5 T. water
1 T. flour
2 c. finely chopped rhubarb

Pour fruit in bottom of 9" pie shell. Mix other ingredients. Pour over fruit. Sprinkle with cinnamon and dot with butter. Bake at 350 degrees for 40-50 minutes or until set. May use blueberries, apple or strawberries.

Mama Ellen's Pecan Pie

1/2 cup sugar
2 Tbsp. flour
2 Tbsp. butter
1/2 tsp salt
3 eggs
1 1/2 cup pecans - chopped
1 cup white Karo Syrup
1 tsp. vanilla

Cream butter and sugar. Add beaten eggs, flour, salt, vanilla and syrup. Stir welland add pecans. Pour mixture into unbaked pie shell and bake approximately 1/2 hour in a moderate oven (250 degrees).

Pecan Pie and Crust Mrs. David (Inez) Smith

3 cups flour
1 cup syrup (white preferred)
1 Tbsp. salt
1 cup sugar
1 cup shortening
1 cup chopped pecans
1/2 cup ice water
3 eggs
1 Tbsp melted butter, pinch of salt and
1 teaspoon vanilla.

Mix shortening and flour until like meal. Put salt in water and mix with flour and shortening until all hold together good. Mix with pastry blender or mixer. This can be kept in refrigerator several days. Roll out for crust. Mix sugar, syrup, eggs, butter, pinch of salt and teaspoon of vanilla. Beat until mixture is just mixed good. Do not over mix. Put pecans in unbaked pie shell and pour syrup mixture over pecans. Bake in 425 degree oven for 10 minutes. Reduce heat to 325 degrees until done (about 15 to 20 minutes).

Mary Ellen's Pecan Pie

2 eggs, well beaten
1/2 c. sugar
1 c. King syrup
pinch of salt
1 t. vanilla
1 c. chopped pecans
2 T. butter, melted

Beat eggs well. Add sugar and syrup. Mix well. Add pecans, butter and vanilla. Mix well. Pour into unbaked pie crust. Bake in moderate, 350 degree, oven for 30-45 minutes until set.

Doris Hicks' Original Chocolate Pie

1/4 cup AP flour
1/2 cup sugar
1 can (12 oz) evaporated milk
1 can Pillsbury milk chocolate frosting (Pillsbury Lovin Lite)
* no longer made

Mix in order listed. Beat until smooth. Add 3/4 cup chopped pecans. 3-4 cup flaked coconut. Stir lightly. Pour in 9 inch deep dish pie crust. Turn up edges. Bake 325 degrees until solid. 35-55 minutes.

This was one of the pies mom loved to make. Mom was a creative cook and liked to experiment with her cooking. It was a challenge to learn to cook from her as she often added this and that and didn't follow recipes. Unfortunately, I don't have this skill and can only cook using detailed recipes.

—Phyllis Hicks Marsh

Mabel's Fresh Strawberry Pie (Diane Hicks Blake)

1 9" baked pie crust
1 quart strawberries (or blueberries or peaches)
1 c. water
1 c. sugar
3 T. strawberry jello (use jello to match fruit)
3 1/2 T. cornstarch
pinch of salt

Mix cornstarch and water together. Add sugar, salt and jello. Works best in nonstick frying pan. Bring to a boil. Stir until like pudding – 2 or 3 minutes, until you cook out the cornstarch taste. Cook (??? cover??) all berries. Cover in cool whip or fresh whipped cream. Place in refrigerator.

Blueberry Pie (or Cherry) (Diane Hicks Blake)

Crust:
1 stick butter
1 c. flour
1 c. chopped pecans
Mix together and press into pie pan; bake at 350 for 20 minutes. Cool.

Filling:
8 oz. cream cheese
1 c. sugar
1 small cool whip

Whip together cream cheese and sugar; fold in cool whip. Fill pie crust with blueberry or cherry pie filling. Cover this with the cream cheese filling. Place in refrigerator. Serve cold. Also freezes well.

Aunt Etta's Pie (Diane Hicks Blake)

Growing up I spent every summer with Aunt Noma and Uncle Harry. This is a pie Aunt Noma made for me.

1 9" unbaked pie crust
Thick applesauce (3 or 4 c.)
3 egg yolks (save whites)
1 1/2 T flour
5 T. sugar
1 t. vanilla

Cream yolks, sugar, flour and vanilla until creamy. Pour applesauce into shell and spread egg mixture over it. Bake at 350 until golden brown. Beat egg whites with 3 T. sugar and 1 t. vanilla. Top baked pie and brown in oven.

Mama Ellen's Old Fashion Coconut Pie

1/2 cup coconut
1/4 cup sugar
1/2 cup milk
2 Tbsp. flour
2 eggs
2 Tbsp. butter
1 tsp. vanilla
pinch of salt

Combine dry ingredients. Beat eggs, add milk and dry ingredients alternately. Add vanilla. Melt butter and add to mixture. Pour into unbaked pie crust. Bake at 300 degrees 45 minutes to 60 minutes.

Carrot Cake Georgia Smith Futrell

2 c. Sugar
1 c. Wesson Oil
4 eggs
2 1/4 c. Self Rising Flour
1 jar baby food carrots
1 t. Baking soda
2 t. cinnamon
dash salt

Icing
1 stick margarine
8 oz cream cheese
1 box confectioners sugar
1 t. vanilla
1/2 c. chopped nuts

Beat together sugar and Wesson oil. Add 4 eggs. Sift together flour, baking sodium cinnamon and salt. Add 1/2 flour and 1 jar baby food carrots at a time. Add vanilla. Bake 30 minutes at 325 degrees.

For icing: beat margarine and cream cheese together and ad confectioners sugar. Note: Leave cream cheese and margarine in refrigerator until ready to beat. Add vanilla and pecans. Spread on three layers.

Mabel's Italian Cream Cake (Diane Hicks Blake)

1 stick butter
1/2 c. crisco
2 c. sugar
5 egg yolks (save whites)
2 c. flour
1 t. soda
1 c. buttermilk
1 t. vanilla
1 c. chopped nuts
1 c. flaked coconut

Grease and flour 3 cake pans. Cream butter, crisco, sugar; add egg yolks. Sift soda with flour and add to mixture alternating buttermilk and flour. Add nuts, coconut and vanilla. Fold in beaten egg whites. Divide into the 3 cake pans and bake at 350 degrees. Cool.

Top with:
1 box 4x powdered sugar
1/2 c. crisco
8 oz. cream cheese

Mix all together.
Everyone made this cake in the 60s. Just as good as pig picking cake.

Doris' Lady Baltimore Cake (Branda Hicks Lane)

1 cup butter
2 cups sugar
3 1/2 cups flour, sifted
1 cup sweet milk
Beaten whites of 6 eggs
3 teaspoons Watkins Baking Powder
1 teaspoon Watkins Vanilla

Cream butter, beat in sugar, add sifted dry ingredients alternately with milk. Fold in stiffly beaten egg whites. Bake in layers in 376 degree oven. Use filling below.

Filling
2 1/2 cups sugar
1/2 cup white corn syrup
1/8 teaspoon salt
1/2 cup water 2 egg whites
1 teaspoon Watkins Vanilla
2/3 cup raisins
2/3 cup nut meats, cut

Cook sugar, syrup, salt, water to thread stage, 246 degrees. Slowly beat hot syrup into stiffly beaten egg whites. Add Watkins Vanilla, then put aside 1 cup of frosting for top of cake. Add fruit, nuts and beat briskly. Spread layers and top of cake filling and cover cake with thin layer of the boiled frosting.

When all the family went to Mama Ellen and Papa Frank's house at Christmas, I remember Mother always made a Lady Baltimore cake. I have searched for her recipe. I think the recipe was in the Watkins Cook Book. The book looks like it had been used many times, especially the page with this recipe. The Watkins salesman would come to the house and Mother would buy vanilla flavoring., etc. I think this is the source of the cookbook.

The recipe doesn't have good directions for how many pans or how to prep pans.

Aunt Ava's Brownies Supreme

2 squares chocolate
1/3 C. Shortening
3/4 C. flour
1/2 t. baking soda
1/2 t. salt
1 C. sugar
1 egg, unbeaten
1 t. vanilla
1/2 C. chopped nuts

Melt chocolate and shortening together over hot water, remove from heat and cool. Sift dry ingredients together and add to chocolate mixture. Beat vigorously for one minute. Add egg and vanilla and beat again for one minute. Stir in nuts, then spread in a well greased 8" square pan. Bake 375 degrees for 25-30 minutes. Cool, then cut in squares. Sprinkle with powdered sugar if desired.

Mary Ellen's Cheese Wafers

2 c. grated sharp cheese
2 sticks butter, room temperature
2 c. plain flour
2 c. Rice krispies
Dash red pepper
1/2 t. salt

Work by hand all ingredients. Roll into small balls place on cookie sheet. Flatten with fork. Bake at 350 degrees for 16 minutes.

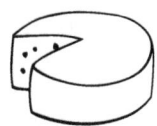

Snicker Doodles (Diane Hicks Blake)

Allen Jr.'s Favorite cookies

1 c. butter
1 1/2 c. sugar
1 egg
1 t. vanilla
2 1/2 c. plain flour
1 t. baking powder
1 t. cream of tartar
1/4 t. salt

Cream butter and sugar, add egg and vanilla; cream until fluffy. Add the dry ingredients. Chill dough about 1/2 hour. Roll into 1" balls. Mix 1/4 c. sugar and 1 t. cinnamon. Roll balls in sugar mixture. Bake at 400 degrees on an ungreased cookie sheet.

Aunt Ava's Sugar Cookies

1 c. sugar
1/2 Tbsp. baking soda
1/2 c. butter
1 tsp. cream of tartar
1 egg
1/2 tsp. salt
2 Tbsp. cold water
2 1/4 cup flour
1 Tbsp. vanilla

Cream sugar and butter together. Add egg and and cream untilvery creamy. Add water and vanilla. Add dry ingredients and mix until smooth. Roll out as thin as wanted — cut and bake at 450 degrees.

Aunt Ava's Nutty Fingers

3 1/4 cup all purpose flour
3/4 cup sugar
1/2 tsp. baking powder
1 1/4 cup softened butter or margarine
1/4 tsp salt
1 c. nuts chopped fine
1 egg

Sift flour, baking powder and salt together. Mix sugar with sugar until creamy. Beat 1 egg. Stir in nuts. Add flour mixture and blend thoroughly. Press dough through cookie press or shape with hands. Make each one about 2 inches long. Bake on ungreased cookie sheet. Bake in hot oven 425 degrees 5 to 8 minutes or until set but not brown. Roll each cookie in powdered sugar.

Aunt Ava's Frozen Cookies

1 cup butter
2 cups all purpose flour
1 cup brown sugar
1/2 tsp soda
1/2 cup white sugar
1 tsp salt
1 egg - beaten well
1 cup chopped nuts
1 tsp vanilla

Cream butter. Gradually add sugar. Continue creaming until mixture islight and fluffy. Add egg and vanilla and mix well. Sift flour, soda, and salt together and gradually add to mixture. Beat well after addition. Add nuts last. Shape in 3/4 inch roll and wrap in waxed paper and freeze. Slice frozen dough 1/8 inch thick and bake on cookie sheet at 375 degrees for 10 to 12 minutes.

Sarah Smith Pate's Frosted Date Balls's (Branda Hicks Lane)

1 1/4 c. sifted all purpose flour
1/4 tsp.salt
1/2 c. butter or shortening
1/3 c. sifted confectioners sugar
1 Tbsp. milk
1 tsp. vanilla
2/3 c. chopped Dromedary Dates
1/2 c. chopped nuts
Confectioners sugar

Combine flour and salt. Sift twice. Cream butter and gradually add sugar. Add milk, vanilla and stir in the sifted flour. Blend in dates and nuts. Roll in 1 inch balls. Place about 3 inches apart on ungreased baking sheet. Bake in 300 degree oven about 20 minutes or until light brown. While still warm, roll in confectioners sugar.
Makes 3 dozen cookies.

This recipe was found in old cookbook published by the Mount Carmel Woman's Society of Christian Service.

Mother's Recipe For Snow Cream

1 large can of Carnation milk
2 eggs
1/8 teaspoon salt
1 cup sugar
1 teaspoon vanilla

Mix sugar and eggs. Add milk, vanilla, salt and mix well. Add as much snow as needed.

This was a real treat when I was a child. With all the pollution in our environment today, I would not make this recipe.
— *Branda Hicks Lane*

Aunt Ava's Jelly Roll

3/4 C. sifted cake flour
3/4 t. baking powder
1/4. t. salt
4 eggs
3/4 c. sugar
1 t. vanilla
1 C. jelly, preferably a tart type

Start oven at 400 degrees or hot and grease a 15" x 10" x 1 1/2" jelly roll pan or similar baking tray, Grease with shortening and line with wax paper.

Sift and measure flour. Mix baking powder, salt, and eggs in large mixing bowl, and beat until they begin to thicken. Add the sugar a little at a time, beating constantly until the mixture is smooth. Add flour and vanilla extract, mixing them in with a gentle folding motion, until batter looks creamy and smooth, pour batter into pan and bake for 13-15 minutes. While cake bakes sprinkle a clean tea towel with a generous coating of confectioners sugar. When cake is finished, turn out on the towel, peel off the wax paper and roll towel, sugar and all up tightly. Let roll cool about 10 minutes, unroll carefully and spread with jelly. Roll again, wrap in towel and cool on a rack.

Ava and Mary Ellen's Fruit Cobbler

1/2 cup milk
1 tsp. baking powder
1 cup flour
1 cup sugar
2 ½ cups any fruit or berries (may use fresh fruit)
3 T. butter

Mix the dry ingredients and add milk, forming a batter. Melt three tablespoons of butter in 2-quart dish. Heat berries or fruit, mixing in a extra ½ cup sugar if fruit and berries are not sweet. Pour batter on top of hot melted butter. Pour hot fruit/berries over batter. Bake at 350° for 35 minutes.

Aunt Ava's Christmas Pudding Candy

3 C. sugar
1 C. light cream
1 heaping T. butter
1 t. vanilla
1 pound dates
1 pound figs
1 pound raisins
1 pound coconut
1 or 2 cups nuts

Cook sugar, cream, and butter until it forms a soft ball when a few drops are dropped in cold water. Beat until creamy, then beat in fruits and nuts. When well mixed, roll as for meat loaf. Wrap in damp cloth, then in wax paper. Let ripen for two weeks in refrigerator. Slice and serve.

Aunt Doris' Divinity

2 1/2 cups sugar
1/2 cup light-colored corn syrup
2 eggs whites (room temperature)
1 teaspoon vanilla
1/2 cup chopped pecans
1/2 cup water

In 2 qt saucepan combine sugar, syrup, and water. Cook and stir over medium-high heat until it boils. Clip candy thermometer to side of pan. Reduce heat to medium. Don't stir mixture and cook to 260 degrees or hard boil stage (10-15 min).

Remove from heat. In large mixing bowl beat egg whites on medium speed of mixer until stiff peaks form. Gradually pour hot mixture in thin stream over whites, beating on high speed for about 3 minutes; scrape sides of bowl occasionally. Add vanilla and continue beating until candy starts to lose its gloss (5-6 min). When beaters are lifted, mixture should fall in a ribbon that mounds on itself. Test it by dropping spoonful of candy onto waxed paper. If it stays mounded, it is ready. If it flattens, beat one minute more and test. Now you can stir in the nuts. Quickly drop mixture onto wax paper. Store tightly covered. Makes about 40 pieces.

** I always have failure if I make this candy on a rainy day. **

Recipe is from my first cookbook — Better Homes and Garden.

At Christmas Mother would buy or make gifts for Phyllis and me. She was an excellent seamstress. She loved to make dresses for us and our dolls. She would sew late at night after we had been tucked in bed. Daddy would buy the tree (Charlie Brown type tree) and our treats. Phyllis would get chocolate covered cherries and I would get cashews. We still have a fondness for these treats.

As an adult I decided to try making divinity, which was one of Daddy's favorites. I had no cooking skills when I married, so I was anxious about making this candy. My first attempt was a success and I made it every year for him. Mother had a sweet tooth too and she would tell Daddy to keep the divinity in the truck so she wouldn't eat it.

— *Branda Hicks Lane*

Homemade Ice Cream

We often made ice cream in the summer when the vegetables were ready in the garden. Daddy would put the yard chairs under the big walnut tree for us to work and to take turns turning the handle on the ice cream freezer. Just thinking about this treat would make shelling peas and shucking corn on those hot days go a little faster.

Ice Cream Recipe

Need 1 gallon hand cranked ice cream freezer
Ice Rock salt
Two 15 oz cans sweetened condensed milk
6 cups milk
2 tablespoons vanilla

Pace sweetened condensed milk in large bowl. Add vanilla and milk. Stir until smooth. Chill. Pour into chilled one gallon freezer container. Put chilled container into ice cream freezer. Pack with ice and salt. Turn until ice cream gets firm. Cover and finish your chores. Take container out, open and remove dasher. Have your bowl and spoon ready to have delicious treat.

— *Branda Hicks Lane*

Family Tree

The Hicks Cousins

Name	Birth Year	Parent
Sarah*	1931	Inez
Janet*	1936	John
Jane*	1937	Inez
Sandra	1938	John
Ray	1940	Casper
Branda	1942	Otto
William Frank*	1943	Casper
Georgia	1944	Inez
Diane	1945	Milton
Alan Scott	1947	George
Phyllis	1948	Otto
Allen Milton*	1948	Milton
Joy	1950	Casper
Johnnie	1951	John
Frank	1954	Mary Ellen
James D	1957	Casper
Carolyn	1957	Mary Ellen
Lisa	1961	Milton

*Deceased

Family Tree Chart

Four-Generation Pedigree

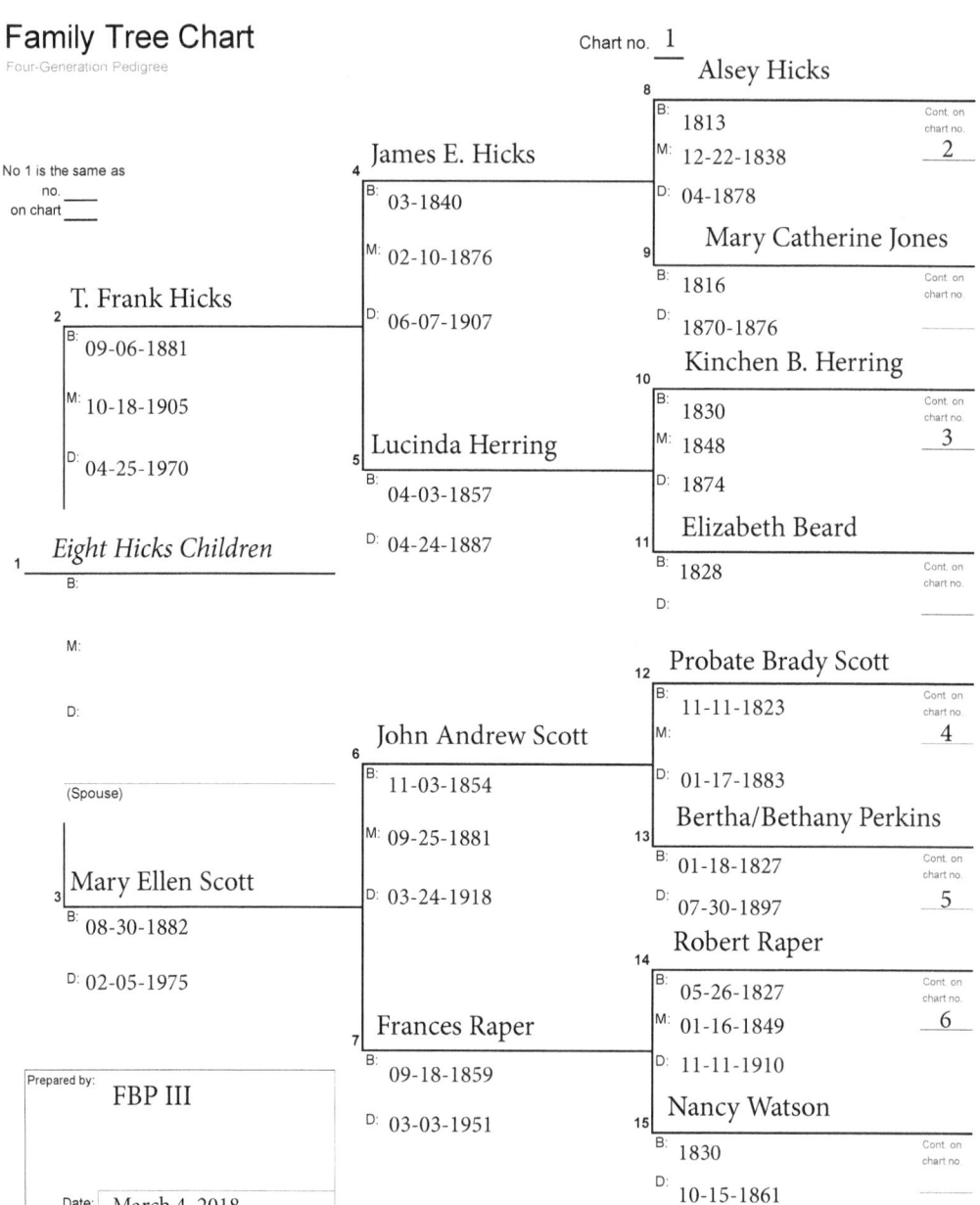

— 108

Family Tree Chart
Four-Generation Pedigree

Chart no. 2

No 1 is the same as
no. 8
on chart 1

1 Alsey Hicks
B: 1813
M: 12-22-1838
D: 04-1878

(Spouse) Mary Catherine Jones

2 James Hicks
B: 1785
M: 05-02-1807
D: 1840-1850

3 Sally Pearson
B: 1785
D: 1840-1850

4 Isaac Hicks (?)
B:
M:
D:

5
B:
D:

6
B:
M:
D:

7
B:
D:

8
B:
M:
D:

9
B:
D:

10
B:
M:
D:

11
B:
D:

12
B:
M:
D:

13
B:
D:

14
B:
M:
D:

15
B:
D:

Prepared by:

Date:

Family Tree Chart
Four-Generation Pedigree

Chart no. 3

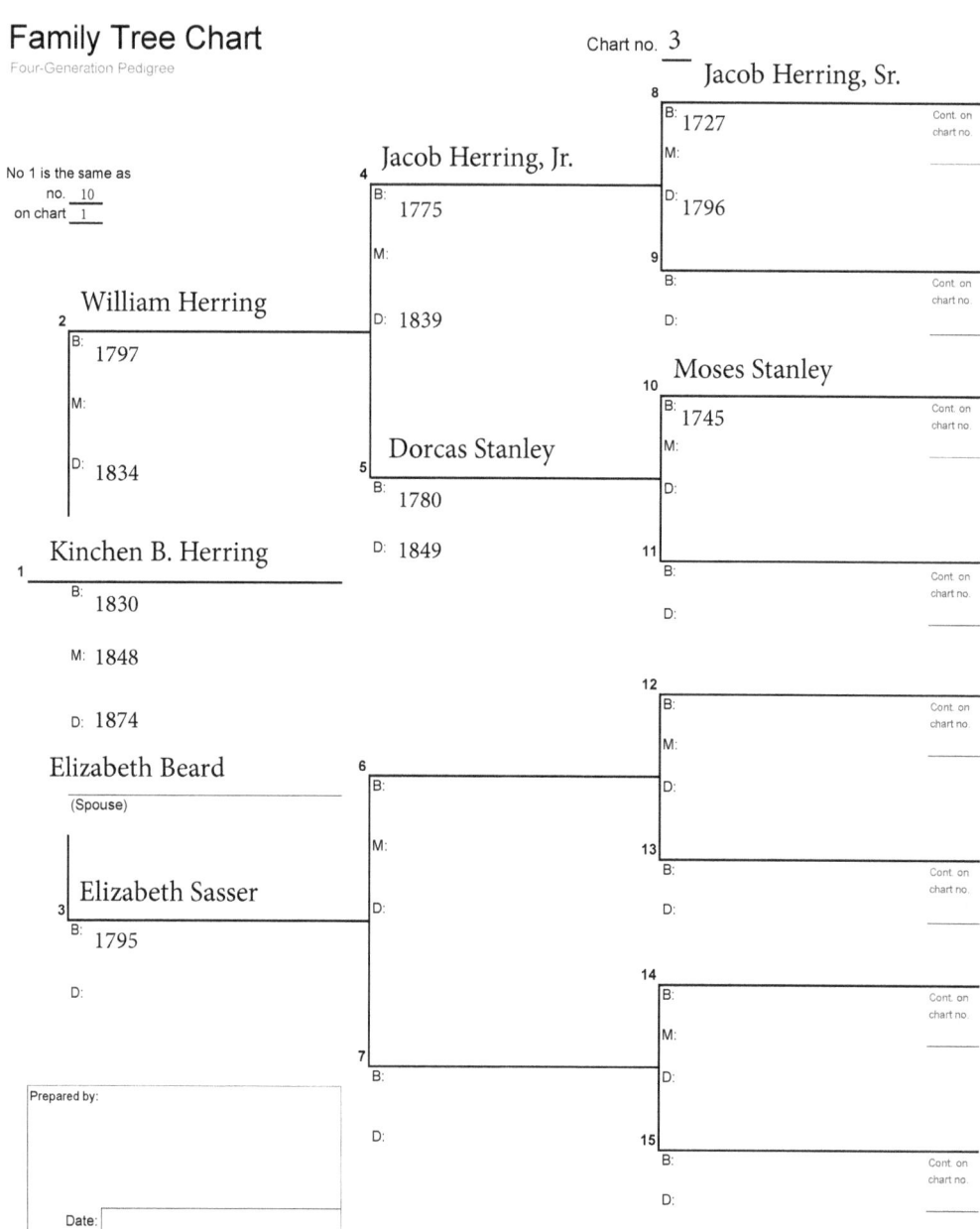

Family Tree Chart
Four-Generation Pedigree

Chart no. 4

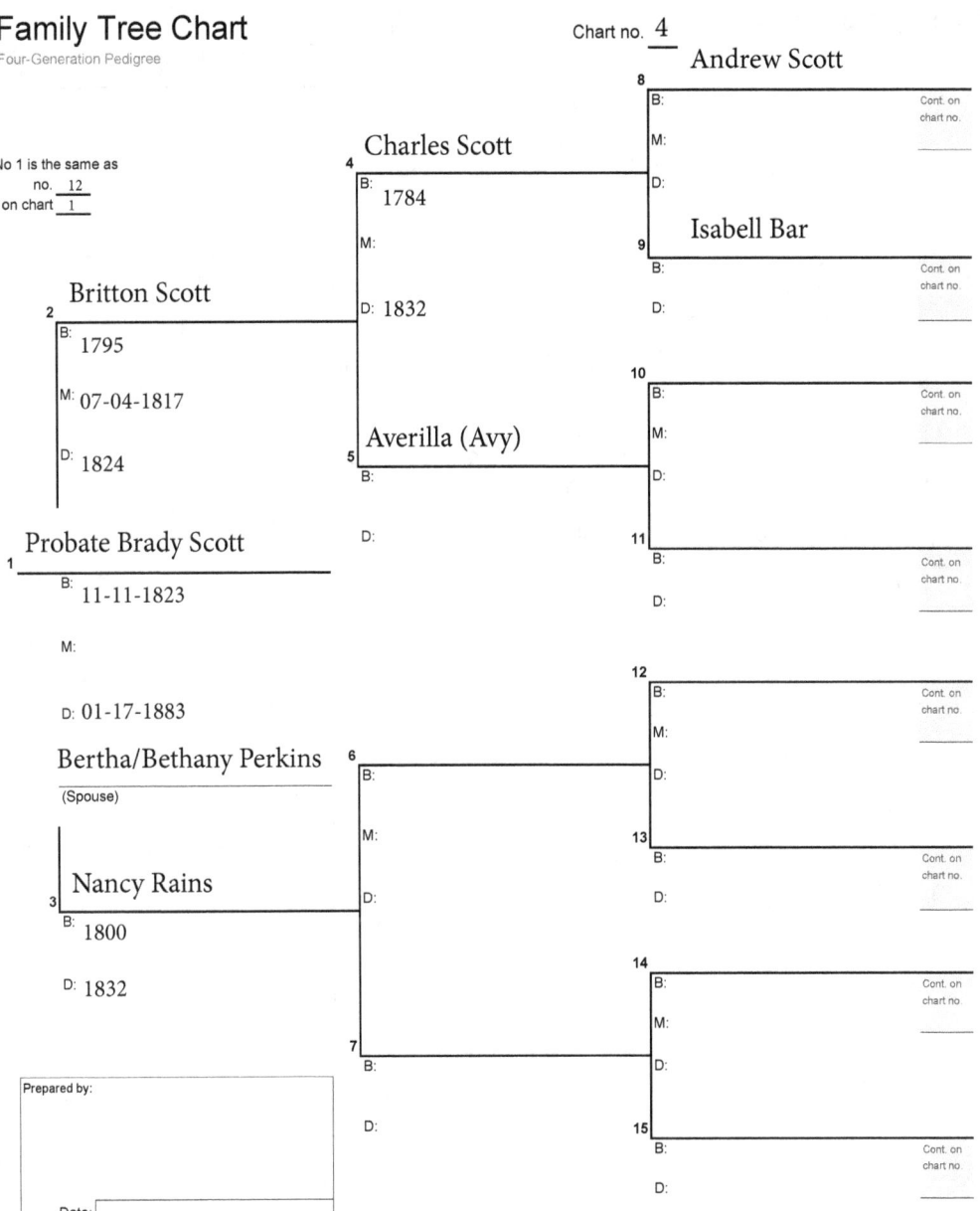

No 1 is the same as no. 12 on chart 1

1 Probate Brady Scott
B: 11-11-1823
M:
D: 01-17-1883

Bertha/Bethany Perkins (Spouse)

2 Britton Scott
B: 1795
M: 07-04-1817
D: 1824

3 Nancy Rains
B: 1800
D: 1832

4 Charles Scott
B: 1784
M:
D: 1832

5 Averilla (Avy)
B:
D:

8 Andrew Scott
B:
M:
D:

9 Isabell Bar
B:
D:

Prepared by:
Date:

— 111

Family Tree Chart
Four-Generation Pedigree

Chart no. 5

No 1 is the same as no. 13 on chart 1

1. Bertha/Bethany Perkins
   B: 01-18-1827
   M:
   D: 07-30-1897
   Spouse: Probate Brady Scott

2. Aaron Perkins
   B: 01-21-1790
   M:
   D: 1843

3. Celia
   B:
   D:

4. Jeremiah Perkins
   B:
   M:
   D:

5. Faithy Loving
   B: 1760
   D: 1820

6.
   B:
   M:
   D:

7.
   B:
   D:

8. David Perkins
   B:
   M:
   D:

9.
   B:
   D:

10.
    B:
    M:
    D:

11.
    B:
    D:

12.
    B:
    M:
    D:

13.
    B:
    D:

14.
    B:
    M:
    D:

15.
    B:
    D:

Prepared by:
Date:

— 112

Family Tree Chart
Four-Generation Pedigree

Chart no. 6

No 1 is the same as
no. 14
on chart 1

1 Robert Raper
B: 05-26-1827
M: 01-16-1849
D: 11-11-1910

Nancy Watson
(Spouse)

2 John Raper
B: 1790
M: 02-07-1814
D: 01-10-1845

3 Elizabeth Sasser
B: 1792
D: 03-15-1862

4 Robert Raper
B: 1757
M:
D: 05-08-1836

5 Nancy Weekes
B: 1761
D: 05-08-1842

6
B:
M:
D:

7
B:
D:

8
B:
M:
D:

9
B:
D:

10
B:
M:
D:

11
B:
D:

12
B:
M:
D:

13
B:
D:

14
B:
M:
D:

15
B:
D:

Prepared by:

Date:

❧ Relationship Chart

Instructions:
1. Identify the most recent common ancestor of the two individuals with the unknown relationship.
2. Determine the common ancestor's relationship to each person (for example, grandparent or great-grandparent).

	parent	grandparent	great-grandparent	great-great-grandparent
parent	siblings	nephew or niece	grandnephew or -niece	great-grandnephew or -niece
grandparent	nephew or niece	first cousins	first cousins once removed	first cousins twice removed
great-grandparent	grandnephew or -niece	first cousins once removed	second cousins	second cousins once removed
great-great-grandparent	great-grandnephew or -niece	first cousins twice removed	second cousins once removed	third cousins
third-great-grandparent	great-great-grandnephew or -niece	first cousins three times removed	second cousins twice removed	third cousins once removed
fourth-great-grandparent	third-great-grandnephew or -niece	first cousins four times removed	second cousins three times removed	third cousins twice removed
fifth-great-grandparent	fourth-great-grandnephew or -niece	first cousins five times removed	second cousins four times removed	third cousins three times removed
sixth-great-grandparent	fifth-great-grandnephew or -niece	first cousins six times removed	second cousins five times removed	third cousins four times removed

3. In the topmost row of the chart, find the common ancestor's relationship to cousin number one. In the far-left column, find the common ancestor's relationship to cousin number two.
4. Trace the row and column from step 3. The square where they meet shows the two individuals' relationship.

third-great-grandparent	fourth-great-grandparent	fifth-great-grandparent	sixth-great-grandparent
great-great-grandnephew or -niece	third-great-grandnephew or -niece	fourth-great-grandnephew or -niece	fifth-great-grandnephew or -niece
first cousins three times removed	first cousins four times removed	first cousins five times removed	first cousins six times removed
second cousins twice removed	second cousins three times removed	second cousins four times removed	second cousins five times removed
third cousins once removed	third cousins twice removed	third cousins three times removed	third cousins four times removed
fourth cousins	fourth cousins once removed	fourth cousins twice removed	fourth cousins three times removed
fourth cousins once removed	fifth cousins	fifth cousins once removed	fifth cousins twice removed
fourth cousins twice removed	fifth cousins once removed	sixth cousins	sixth cousins once removed
fourth cousins three times removed	fifth cousins twice removed	sixth cousins once removed	seventh cousins

www.ingramcontent.com/pod-product-compliance
Lightning Source LLC
Chambersburg PA
CBHW070050230426
43661CB00005B/840